KT-414-467

The "Teaching of English" Series

General Editor—Sir Henry Newbolt

A BOOK OF ESCAPES AND HURRIED JOURNEYS

No. 14

THE MARQUIS OF MONTROSE

From a pen-drawing by
Russell Reeve

A BOOK of ESCAPES and Hurried Journeys

BY

JOHN BUCHAN

THOMAS NELSON & SONS, Ltd.
LONDON, EDINBURGH, AND NEW YORK

First Edition in this Series published May 1925.
Reprinted August, October, 1925 ; April 1926 ;
March 1927 ; August 1928.

PREFACE

I HAVE never yet seen an adequate definition of Romance, and I am not going to attempt one. But I take it that it means in the widest sense that which affects the mind with a sense of wonder—the surprises of life, fights against odds, weak things confounding strong, beauty and courage flowering in unlikely places. In this book we are concerned with only a little plot of a great province, the efforts of men to cover a certain space within a certain limited time under an urgent compulsion, which strains to the uttermost body and spirit.

Why is there such an eternal fascination about tales of hurried journeys? In the great romances of literature they provide many of the chief dramatic moments, and, since the theme is common to Homer and the penny reciter, it must appeal to a very ancient instinct in human nature. The truth seems to be that we live our lives under the twin categories of time and space, and that when the two come into conflict we get the great moment. Whether failure or success is the result, life is sharpened, intensified, idealized. A long journey even with the most lofty purpose may be a dull thing to read of, if it is made at leisure; but a hundred yards may be a breathless business if only a few seconds are granted to complete it. For then it becomes a "sporting event," a race; and the interest which makes millions read of the Derby is the same in a grosser form as that with which we follow an expedition straining to relieve a beleaguered fort, or a man fleeing to sanctuary with the avenger behind him.

I have included "escapes" in my title, for the conflict of space and time is of the essence of all escapes, since the escaper is either pursued or in instant danger of pursuit. But, as a matter of fact, many escapes are slow affairs and their interest lies rather in ingenuity than in speed. Such in fiction is the escape of Dantès in *Monte Cristo* from the dungeons of Chateau d'If, and in history the laborious tunnelling performances of some of the prisoners in the American Civil War. The escapes I have chosen are, therefore, of a special type—the hustled kind, where there has been no time to spare, and the pursuer has either been hot-foot on the trail or the fugitive has moved throughout in an atmosphere of imminent peril.

It is, of course, in the operations of war that one looks for the greater examples. The most famous hurried journeys have been made by soldiers—by Alexander, Hannibal, and Julius Cæsar; by Marlborough in his dash to Blenheim; by Napoleon many times; by Sir John Moore in his retreat to Corunna; by a dozen commanders in the Indian Mutiny; by Stonewall Jackson and Jeb Stuart in their whirlwind rides; by the fruitless expedition to relieve Gordon. But the operations of war are a little beside my purpose. In them the movement is, as a rule, only swift when compared with the normal pace of armies, and the cumbrousness and elaboration of the military machine lessen the feeling of personal adventure. I have included only one march of an army—Montrose's, because his army was such a little one, its speed so amazing and its purpose so audacious, that its swoop upon Inverlochy may be said to belong to the class of personal exploits. For a different reason I have included none of the marvellous escapes of the Great War. These are in a world of their own, and some day I may make a book of them.

I have retold the stories, which are all strictly true, using the best evidence I could find and, in the case of the older ones, often comparing a dozen authorities. For the account of Prince Charlie's wanderings I have to thank my friend Professor Rait of Glasgow, the Historiographer Royal for Scotland. My aim has been to include the widest varieties of fateful and hasty journey, extending from the hundred yards or so of Lord Nithsdale's walk to the Tower Gate to the 4,000 miles of Lieutenants Parer and M'Intosh, from the ride of the obscure Dick King to the flights of princes, from the midsummer tragedy of Marie Antoinette to the winter comedy of Princess Clementina.

J. B.

Alexander.

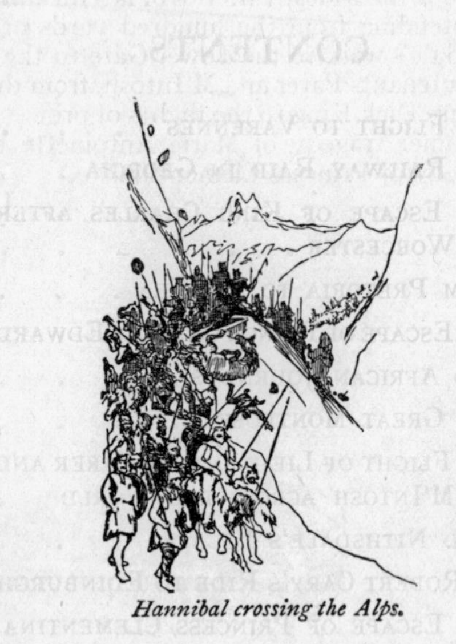

Hannibal crossing the Alps.

CONTENTS

Aristocrats.
(French Revolution.)

A BOOK OF ESCAPES AND HURRIED JOURNEYS

I

THE FLIGHT TO VARENNES

I

On the night of Monday, 20th June, in the year 1791, the baked streets of Paris were cooling after a day of cloudless sun. The pavements were emptying and the last hackney coaches were conveying festive citizens homewards. In the Rue de l'Echelle, at the corner where it is cut by the Rue St. Honoré, and where the Hôtel de Normandie stands to-day, a hackney carriage, of the type which was then called a "glass coach," stood waiting by the kerb. It stood opposite the door of one Ronsin, a saddler, as if expecting a fare; but the windows were shuttered, and the honest Ronsin had gone to bed. On the box sat a driver in the ordinary clothes of a coachman, who while he waited took snuff with other cabbies, and with much good-humoured chaff declined invitations to drink.

The hour of eleven struck; the streets grew emptier and darker; but still the coach waited. Presently from the direction of the Tuileries came a hooded lady with two hooded children, who, at a nod from the driver, entered the coach. Then came another veiled lady attended by a servant, and then a stout male figure with a wig and a round hat, who, as he passed the sentries at the palace gate, found his shoe-buckle undone and bent to fasten it, thereby hiding his face. The glass coach was now nearly full; but still the driver waited.

The little group of people all bore famous names. On the box, in the driver's cloak, sat Count Axel Fersen, a young Swedish nobleman who had vowed his life to the service of the Queen of France. The first hooded lady, whose passport proclaimed that she was a Russian gentlewoman, one Baroness de Korff, was the Duchess de Tourzel, the governess of the royal children. The other hooded lady was no other than Madame Elizabeth, the King's sister. One of the children was the little Princess Royal, afterwards known as the Duchess d'Angoulême; the other, also dressed like a girl, was the Dauphin. The stout gentleman in the round hat was King Louis XVI. The coach in the Rue de l'Echelle was awaiting the Queen.

For months the royal family had been prisoners in the Tuileries, while the Revolution marched forward in swift stages. They were prisoners in the strictest sense, for they had been forbidden even the customary Easter visit to St. Cloud. The puzzled, indolent king was no better than a cork tossed upon yeasty waters. Mirabeau was dead—Mirabeau who might have saved the monarchy; now the only hope was to save the royal family, for the shades were growing very dark around it. Marie Antoinette, the Queen, who, as Mirabeau had said, was "the only man the King had about him," had resolved to make a dash for freedom. She would leave Paris, even France, and seek her friends beyond the borders. The National Militia and the National Guards were for the Revolution; but the army of Bouillé on the eastern frontier, composed largely of German mercenaries, would do its general's orders, and Bouillé was staunch for the crown. Count

Fersen had organized the plan, and the young Duke de Choiseul, a nephew of the minister of Louis XV., had come to Paris to settle the details. A coach had been built for the journey, a huge erection of leather and wood, of the type then called a berline, painted yellow, upholstered in white velvet, and drawn by no less than eleven horses. It was even now standing outside the eastern gate, and Fersen was waiting with his hackney carriage to conduct the royal fugitives thither.

But where was the Queen? Marie Antoinette, dressed as a maid and wearing a broad gipsy hat, had managed to pass the palace doors; but rumours had got abroad, and even as she stood there leaning on a servant's arm the carriage of Lafayette dashed up to the arch, for he had been summoned by the Commandant, who represented the eyes of the National Assembly. The sight flurried her, and she and her servant took the wrong turning. They hastened towards the river, and then back, but found no waiting coach.

The chimes struck midnight, and at long last Fersen from the box in the Rue de l'Echelle saw the figure which he knew so well, the lady in the gipsy hat who was the Queen. The party was now complete. The door was shut; the driver plied his whip, and the coach started northward through the sleeping city. Up the street where Mirabeau had lived they went, till in the Rue de Clichy the coachman stopped to ask a question at a house about the great berline. He was told that it had left half an hour ago. The carriage then turned eastward and passed through the eastern gate. There stood the berline, with two yellow liveried gentlemen of the Guard to act as postilions.

The King and Queen, the two children, Madame Elizabeth, and the so-called Baroness de Korff, free now from the cramped hackney coach, reclined at ease on the broad cushions. The hackney coach was then turned adrift citywards, and was found next morning upset in a ditch. Again Count Fersen took the reins, and as the eastern sky was paling to dawn they reached the end of the first stage, the post and relay station of Bondy.

Fresh horses were waiting and fresh postilions, and one of the gentlemen-in-waiting took Fersen's place on the box. Fersen walked round to the side where the Queen sat and took a brief farewell. Marie Antoinette's hand touched his and slipped upon his finger a broad ring of very pale gold. The young Swede turned and rode towards Bourget and the highway to Brussels, so passing out of the history of France.

II

Daylight broadened and the great berline rumbled along the highroad, being presently joined by a cabriolet carrying two of the Queen's maids and a collection of baggage. The royal family, no longer drowsy in the fresh morning air, fell into good spirits. A matter of an hour and a half had been wasted at the start, but now the coach travelled briskly at a speed of something like seven miles an hour. They believed the escape to have already succeeded, and talked happily of their plans. Soon the suburbs and the market gardens were left behind, and long before they reached the posting station of Meaux they were in a land of deep meadows and cornfields.

Their plan was to go by way of Châlons, Ste. Menehould, and Clermont to Varennes, where Bouillé would await them. But meantime cavalry patrols from Bouillé's army were to come west into Champagne and be ready at each stage to form up behind and make a screen between them and their enemies. The weak points of the scheme are clear. Had the royal family divided itself and gone by different routes to the frontier in humbler equipages there would have been little risk of capture. But a coach so vast as the new

King and Queen were in flight; they were going towards Metz!

The ex-dragoon was a man of strong resolution and quick action. The drums were beat; Dandoins and his troop were arrested and disarmed, and with another old dragoon of Condé, one Guillaume, an innkeeper, Drouet set off hell-for-leather on the trail.

The great coach with its eleven horses and its yellow-liveried guards on the rumble, climbed slowly up to the summit of the Argonne ridge. There were about 400 feet to climb, and it was some four miles to the crest. After that came the little village of Islettes in a hollow, and then a stretch of four miles to the town of Clermont in the valley of the river Aire. There the royal road must turn at right angles down the Aire to Varennes, which lay nine miles off, a flat straight road in the valley bottom. Drouet and Guillaume had the last two horses left in Ste. Menehould, and the berline had an hour's start of them. They believed that the King was going to Metz, and that what was before them was a stern chase on the highroad.

The berline reached Clermont about twenty minutes to ten. At Clermont there were royal troops, and Drouet had no notion how to deal with them; but he hoped somehow to raise the people in the town on his side. The occupants of the berline had now lost all their high hopes of the morning. They realized that they were late and that somehow their plans were miscarrying, and they were in a fever to get past Varennes into the protection of Bouillé's army. It took a quarter of an hour to change horses at Clermont, and then about ten o'clock the Metz road was relinquished and the great vehicle lumbered off at its best pace down the Aire valley.

About the same moment Drouet and Guillaume came within a mile of Clermont. The night had grown very dark and cloudy, though there was somewhere a moon. They heard voices and discovered it was the postilions from Ste. Menehould turning homewards. These postilions had a story to tell. The berline was not on the Metz road. They had heard the orders given to turn northward to Varennes.

Drouet was a man of action, and in a moment his mind was made up. He must somehow get ahead of the royal carriage which was on the road in the valley below. The only chance was to cut off the corner by taking to the woody ridge of the Argonne, which stretched some 300 feet above the open plain. Now along that eastern scarp of the Argonne runs a green ride which had once been a Roman road. He and his companion galloped through the brushwood till they struck the ride.

It was, as Carlyle has called it, "a night of spurs." Three parties were straining every nerve to reach Varennes: the anxious King and Queen in the great berline, jolting along the highway; the Duke de Choiseul, who had taken a short cut from Somme-Vesle, avoiding Ste. Menehould, plunging with his hussars among the pathless woods; and Drouet and Guillaume making better speed along the green ride, while from the valley on their right the night wind brought them the far-off sound of the King's wheels. There seemed still a good chance of escape, for at Varennes was Bouillé's son with more hussars, waiting in that part of the village which lay east of the Aire bridge.

Seven miles after he left the highway Drouet came to an ancient stone set up in the forest which bears the name of the Dead Girl—a place only too famous in the Argonne fighting in the Great War. There he took the green ride to the right, and coming out of the woods saw the lights of Varennes a little before him. The town seemed strangely quiet. He and Guillaume had done eleven miles of rough going within an hour; now it was only eleven, and as they stopped to rest their panting beasts they listened for the sound of wheels. But there was no sound. Had the berline with its fateful load beaten them and crossed the bridge into the protection of Bouillé's men?

IV

Drouet rushed into the taverns to ask if any late revellers had seen a great coach go through. The revellers shook their heads. No coach that night had passed through Varennes. Suddenly came a cry, and he looked behind him up the long hill of the Clermont road. There, on the top, were the headlights of the coach. It halted, for it was expecting Bouillé's escort. The Clermont postilions were giving trouble; they declared that they were not bound to go down the hill, for the horses were needed early next morning to carry in the hay. At last the coach started, and the creak of its brakes could be heard on the hill. Drouet ran into the inn called "The Golden Arm," crying on every man who was for France to come out and stop the berline, since inside it was the King.

There was only one thing for him to do, to hold the bridge over the Aire. Now, at the bridgehead stood a great furniture van without horses, waiting to start for somewhere in the morning. Drouet and his handful of assistants pulled it across the bridge and blocked the approach. Meantime one Sausse, a tallow chandler and the procurator of the town, had appeared on the scene, and seen to the rousing of every household on the west side of the river.

Half-way down the hill to the bridge the road goes through an archway under an old church. At that archway the only two men of the company who had arms took up position, and when the berline arrived challenged it and brought it to a stand. Passports were demanded, and as the Baroness de Korff fumbled for them the Queen looked out of the window. She begged the gentlemen, whoever they might be, to get the business over quickly, as "she was desirous of reaching the end of her journey as soon as might be." It was an ill-omened phrase which was long remembered.

Meantime the two armed men had increased their numbers, and some of Bouillé's German hussars joined the crowd, more or less drunk. The cabriolet had also been stopped and the maids in it hustled into the inn. But it seemed that the passports were in order, and the Varennes officials were prepared to let the coach continue on its way. It was the crisis of the French monarchy. Escape seemed once more certain, when Drouet intervened. He knew that Bouillé's son was waiting beyond the river, and that Bouillé himself would arrive soon after dawn with ample forces. What he sought to gain was time; on no account must the King cross the Aire till morning.

The embarrassed officials yielded to his threats and fury. "If there is any doubt," said the procurator, "it will do no harm to wait for daylight. It is a dark night and the beasts are tired." He would endorse the passports in the morning. He assisted the King and the Queen to alight, and escorted them to his own house. Hope was not yet wholly gone, for there were still Choiseul and his hussars blundering through the Argonne woods. Meantime the fierce Drouet had had the tocsin sounded and every soul in Varennes was in the streets, waiting on some happening, they knew not what.

Just about dawn Choiseul arrived with his German troopers. He saw what was astir, and had he had Frenchmen in his command all might have been saved. He urged them to rescue the King, and ordered them to charge to clear the streets, which they did, and formed up outside M. Sausse's house, in which Marie Antoinette and her two children were lying huddled on truckle beds. Outside was the perpetual noise of drums and men; every one who could find any kind of weapon trooped up to it and thronged the square. Meantime, young Bouillé across the river had heard the tocsin, and, being uncertain what to do, had returned to his father.

When the morning light broadened the whole neighbourhood was gathered outside the procurator's house. M. Sausse, a devotee of official decorum, felt compelled to endorse the passports and let the royal family continue their journey. But Drouet had other views, and these views were shared by the crowds in the streets. Choiseul, had his mercenaries been of any value, had still the game in his hands. For the second time he ordered them to charge. But the German hussars, comprehending nothing except that there was a large number of formidable citizens opposed to them, sat still on their horses. The King in his green coat appeared at the window of his lodging and was greeted with cheers and with something else which meant the ruin of his hopes, for the mob of ten thousand with one voice shouted "Back to Paris!"

About six o'clock there arrived at Varennes two men from the Council in Paris, Bayon and Romeuf. They had ridden madly all day and night, and had brought a demand from the Council for their Majesties' immediate return. The Queen was furious, and flung the message on the ground. But the King had made up his mind. He had had enough of this undignified secrecy and uncomfortable jolting. He would go back to Paris to the people with whom he was so popular.

Indeed, he had no other choice. The advance guards of Bouillé's horse were even then appearing on the heights behind the Aire, but there were 10,000 men in Varennes, and nothing but artillery could have cleared the place. Bouillé, even had he been in time, could have done nothing. When, about seven o'clock, the royalist general himself looked down on the bridge, he saw a cloud of dust on the Clermont road which told him that the berline had begun its return journey, accompanied by thousands of marching citizens. The adventure was over. What had seemed so certain had shipwrecked on a multitude of blunders and the strange perversities of fortune. The King and Queen were returning to a prison from which there was to be no outlet but death.

V

What of the young Swede, Count Axel Fersen, whom we last saw at Bondy receiving from Marie Antoinette the broad gold ring? The lovers of queens have for the most part been tragically fated, and his lot was no exception to the rule. It is hard for us to-day to judge of the charm of Marie Antoinette; from her portraits her figure and features seem too heavy, though her hair and colouring were beautiful; but she seems to have had a share of that inexplicable compelling power which certain women have possessed —Helen of Troy, Cleopatra, Mary of Scots, Elizabeth of Bohemia—which makes men willing to ride on their behalf over the edge of the world. Fersen, who had worshipped her at first sight when a boy in his teens, was to spend the nineteen remaining years of his life a slave of tragic and tender memories. After her death he became a "fey" man, silent, abstracted, grave beyond other men, and utterly contemptuous of danger, one like Sir Palamede—

> "Who, riding ever through a lonely world,
> Whene'er on adverse shield or helm he came
> Against the danger desperately hurled,
> Crying her name."

He rose to be a famous soldier and marshal of the Swedish armies, and at the age of fifty-five was confronted with a riot in Stockholm. Inside the church of Riddenholm were the nobles of Sweden, barricaded and safe; outside on the steps he stood alone, having been dragged from his carriage, his sword in his right hand and on his left the ring of the Queen of France, which the people of the North believed to be a thing of witchcraft.

For a little he held the steps, for no man dared come within the sweep of his terrible sword or the glow of his more terrible ring. At last some one thought of stones. They were flung from a distance, and presently he was maimed and crushed till he died. Then, and not till then, the mob came near his body, shielding their eyes from the gleam of the ring. One man, a fisherman, Zaffel by name, took his axe and hacked the finger off while the crowd cheered. Averting his head he plucked at the thing, and, running to the river bank, flung it far into the stream.

The rest of the story of the ring is as wild a legend as ever came out of the North. It is said that Zaffel, going fishing next morning after the fury of the riots was over, came into a lonely reach of water and found his boat standing still. He looked up at the masthead, and there, clasping it, saw a hand lacking one finger. The mutilated hand forced the boat forward against tide and wind, and when he tried the tiller he found that the tiller had no effect upon the course. All day he sat in the boat shivering with terror, till in the cold twilight he saw in front of him a white rock in the stream, and upon a ledge of it Fersen's ring. He took it and glanced up at the masthead. The hand had now recovered its lost finger and had disappeared, and his boat was free once more to obey his direction.

In the early dawn of the next day he was back at Stockholm, babbling nonsense and singing wild songs, beyond doubt a madman. At that moment in the Riddenholm church the nobles, who had left Fersen to die, were gathered round his coffin in the act of burial. Suddenly something glimmered in the dark folds of the pall, and they saw with terror that it was the Queen's ring. When the coffin was lowered into the grave the gravediggers dared not fling earth upon the jewel. They feared that the dead man's spirit would haunt them, so they gave the ring to Fersen's family, with whom it remains to this day.

Marie Antoinette.

II

THE RAILWAY RAID IN GEORGIA

THE time is the spring of 1862, the second year of the American Civil War. The scene is the State of Tennessee; the Confederates are concentrating at Corinth, Mississippi, and the two Northern forces of Grant and Buell are moving on that spot. A month before Grant had won the important action of Fort Donelson. A month later he was to win the battle of Shiloh.

In Buell's army was General O. M. Mitchel, commanding the Northern forces in Middle Tennessee and protecting Nashville with a force of some 17,000 men. Now, President Lincoln especially desired that Eastern Tennessee should be cleared of the enemy, since it was one of the latter's chief supply grounds. General Mitchel believed that Corinth would soon fall, and that the next movement would be eastward towards Chattanooga, that key-point on the Tennessee river which was later the scene of one of Grant's most famous victories. He thought, rightly, that if he could press into the enemy's country and occupy strategical points ahead, he would pave the way for Grant's march eastward.

On the 8th of April the Northerners won the battle of Pittsburg Landing. Next day Mitchel marched south from Shelbyville into Alabama and seized Huntsville. From there he sent a detachment westward to open up communication with the Northern troops at Pittsburg Landing. On the same day he himself took another detachment seventy miles by rail and arrived without difficulty within thirty miles of Chattanooga, two hours from the key position in the West. There, however, he stuck fast, and the capture of Chattanooga was delayed for two years. He failed because another plan had failed, the plan which is the subject of this story.

Chattanooga at the moment was practically without a garrison; but in Georgia there were ample Confederate troops, and the Georgia State Railway and the East Tennessee Railway could bring them up in great force at short notice. If Mitchel was to seize and hold Chattanooga, these lines must be cut for long enough to enable him to consolidate his position. Now, in his army was a certain spy of the name of James J. Andrews, one of these daring adventurers who, in the civil war of volunteers, many of whom were as yet without regular uniforms, could perform exploits impossible in a normal campaign. Andrews conceived the idea of a raid on the Confederate railways, and Mitchel approved. Before he left Shelbyville he authorized Andrews to take twenty-four men, enter the enemy's territory and burn the bridges on the vital railways.

The men were selected from three Ohio regiments, and told only that they were required for secret and dangerous service. They exchanged their uniforms for the ordinary dress worn by civilians in the South, and carried no arms except revolvers. On the 7th of April, by a roadside a mile east of Shelbyville, in the late evening, they met Andrews, who told them his plan. In small detachments of three or four they were to go east into the Cumberland Mountains and work southward, and on the evening of the third day rendezvous with Andrews at Marietta in Georgia, more than 200 miles distant. If any one asked them questions they were to declare that they were Kentuckians going to join the Confederate army.

The weather was bad and the travellers were much delayed by swollen streams. This led Andrews to believe that Mitchel's column would also be delayed, so he sent secret word to the different groups that the attempt would be postponed one day, from Friday to Saturday, 12th April. Of the little party one lost his road and never arrived at the destination; two reached Marietta, but missed the rendezvous; and two were captured and forced into the Confederate army. Twenty, however, early on the morning of Saturday, 12th April, met in Andrews' room at the Marietta Hotel.

They had travelled from Chattanooga as ordinary passengers on the Georgia State Railway. The sight of that railway impressed them with the difficulties of their task, for it was crowded with trains and soldiers. In order to do their work they must capture an engine, but the station where the capture was to be made—Big Shanty—had recently been made a Confederate Camp. Their job was, therefore, to seize an engine in a camp with soldiers all round them, to run it from one to two hundred miles through enemy country, and to dodge or overpower any trains they might meet—no small undertaking for a score of men. Some were in favour of abandoning the enterprise, but Andrews stuck stubbornly to his purpose. He gave his final instructions, and the twenty proceeded to the ticket office to purchase tickets for different stations on the line to Chattanooga.

For eight miles they rode in comfort as passengers, till at Big Shanty they saw the Confederate tents in the misty morning. It had been a drizzling April dawn, and a steady rain was now beginning. The train stopped at Big Shanty for breakfast, and this gave them their chance, for the conductor, the engine-driver, and most of the passengers descended for their meal, leaving the train unguarded.

Among the twenty were men who understood the stoking and driving of railway engines, and it did not take long to uncouple three empty vans, the locomotive, and the tender. Brown and Knight, the two engineers, and the fireman climbed into the cab, and the rest clambered into the rear goods van—no easy job, for the cars stood on a high bank. A sentry with rifle in hand stood not a dozen feet from the engine, watching the whole proceedings, but no move was made until it was too late. Andrews gave the signal, the wheels slipped at first on the greasy metals, and then the train moved forward; and before the uproar in the station behind began it had gathered speed.

The first and worst problem was the passing of trains coming from the north. There were two trains on the time-table which had to be passed at certain stations, and there was also a local goods train not scheduled, which might be anywhere. Andrews hoped to avoid the danger of collision by running according to the schedule of the train he had captured, until the goods train was passed, and then to increase to topmost speed till he reached the Oostenaula and Chickamauga bridges, burn them and pass on through Chattanooga to Mitchel as he moved up from Huntsville. He hoped to reach his chief early in the afternoon.

It was a perfectly feasible plan, and it would almost certainly have been carried out but for that fatal day's delay. On Friday, the day originally fixed, all the trains had been up to time, and the weather had been good; but on that Saturday, as luck would have it, the whole railway was in disorder, every train was late, and two "extras" had been put on, of which the leader had no notion. Had he known this, even a man of his audacity would scarcely have started, and the world would have been the poorer by the loss of a stirring tale.

The party had to make frequent stops, particularly between stations, to tear up the track, cut the telegraph wires, and load on sleepers to be used for bridge burning; and also at wayside stations to take on wood and water. At the latter Andrews bluffed the officials by telling them that he was one of General Beauregard's officers, and was running a powder train through to that General at Corinth. Unfortunately he had no proper instruments for pulling up the rails, and it was important to keep to the schedule of the captured train, so they tore light-heartedly past towns and villages, trusting to luck, and exhilarated by the successful start of their wild adventure.

At a station called Etowah they found the "Yonah," an old engine owned by an iron company, standing with steam up; but their mind was all on the local goods train, so they left it untouched. Thirty miles on from Big Shanty they reached Kingston, where a branch line entered from the town of Rome. On the branch a train was waiting for the mail—that is to say, their captured train—and Andrews learned that the local goods was expected immediately; so he ran on to a side track, and waited for it.

Presently it arrived, and to the consternation of the little party it carried a red flag to show that another train was close behind it. Andrews marched boldly across to its conductor and asked what was the meaning of the railway being blocked in this fashion, when he had orders to take the powder straight through to General Beauregard? In reply he was told that Mitchel had captured Huntsville and was said to be marching on Chattanooga, and that everything was being cleared out of that town. Andrews ordered him to move his train down the line out of the way, and he obeyed.

It seemed an eternity to the party before the

"extra" arrived, and to their dismay when it turned up they saw that it bore another red flag. The reason given was that it was too heavy for one engine and had therefore to be made up into two sections. So began another anxious wait. The little band—Andrews with the engine-drivers and fireman in the cab, and the rest taking the place of Beauregard's ammunition in the goods vans—had to preserve composure as best they could, with three trains clustered round them and every passenger in the three extremely curious about the mysterious powder train into which the morning mail had been transformed. For one hour and five minutes they waited at Kingston, the men in the goods vans being warned by Andrews to be ready to fight in case of need. He himself kept close to the station in case some mischief-maker should send an inquiring telegram down the line. At long last came the second half of the local, and as soon as it passed the end of their side track the adventurers moved on.

But the alarm had now been raised behind them. From the midst of the confusion at Big Shanty two men set out on foot along the track to make some effort to capture the Northerners. They were railwaymen—one the conductor of the train, W. A. Fuller, and the other a foreman of the Atlanta railway machine shops, called Anthony Murphy. They found a hand-car and pushed forward on it till they reached Etowah, where they realized that the line had been cut by pitching headforemost down the embankment into a ditch. A little thing like this did not dismay them, and at Etowah they found the "Yonah," the iron company's old locomotive, which, as we know, was standing with steam up. They got on board, filled it up with soldiers who happened to be near, and started off at full speed for Kingston, where they were convinced they would catch the filibusters. The "Yonah" actually entered Kingston station four minutes after Andrews had started, and was of course immediately confronted with the three long trains facing the wrong way. It would have taken too long to move them, so the "Yonah" was abandoned, and Murphy uncoupled the engine and one coach of the Rome train, and continued the chase. It was now any one's race. Andrews and his merry men were only a few minutes ahead.

Four miles north from Kingston the little party again stopped and cut the wires. They started to take up a rail and were pulling at the loosened end, when to their consternation they heard behind them the whistle of an engine. They managed to break the rail and then clambered in and moved on. At the next station, Adairsville, they found a mixed goods and passenger train waiting, and learned that there was an express on the road. It was a crazy risk to take, but they dared not delay, so they started at a terrific speed for the next station, Calhoun, hoping to reach it before the express, which was late, could arrive.

They did the nine miles to Calhoun in less than nine minutes, and saw in front of them the express just starting. Hearing their whistle it backed, and enabled them to take a side track, but it stopped in such a manner as to close the other end of the switch. There stood the trains side by side, almost touching each other. Naturally questions were asked, and Andrews was hard put to it to explain. He told the powder story, and demanded in the name of General Beauregard that the other train should at once let him pass. With some difficulty its conductor was persuaded, and moved forward.

They were saved by the broken rail. The pursuit saw it in time and reversed their engine. Leaving the soldiers behind, Fuller and Murphy ran along the track till they met the train which Andrews had passed at Adairsville. They made it back in pursuit, and at Adairsville dropped the coaches and continued with only the locomotive and tender, both loaded with a further complement of armed soldiers. They thought that their quarry was safe at Calhoun, but they reached that place a minute or two after Andrews had moved out.

Everything now depended on whether the band of twenty could make another gap in the track in time, for if they could the road was clear before them to Chattanooga. A few minutes ahead of them was the Oostenaula bridge, and if that could be burned they would soon be safe in Mitchel's camp.

But the mischief was that they had no proper tools, and the taking up of the rails was terribly slow. Once again they heard the whistle of a locomotive behind them and saw their pursuer with armed men aboard. Another minute would have removed the rail, and their victory would have been assured ; but they could do nothing more than bend it, and were compelled to hurry back to their engine.

Now began one of the most astounding hunts on record. At all costs Andrews must gain a little time so as to set fire to the Oostenaula bridge ; so he dropped first one car and then another. The pursuing engine, however, simply picked them up and pushed them ahead of it. There was no time to do anything at the bridge. Over its high trestles they tore, with Fuller and his soldiers almost within rifle shot.

Soon it appeared that there was no difference in the pace of the two engines. The Confederates could not overtake the filibusters, and Fuller's policy was therefore to keep close behind so as to prevent Andrews damaging the track and taking on wood and water. Both engines were driven to their last decimal of power, and Andrews succeeded in keeping his distance. But he was constantly delayed, for he was obliged to cut the telegraph wires after every station he passed, in order that an alarm might not be sent ahead ; and he could not stop long enough to tear up rails.

All that man could do in the way of obstruction he did, for at all costs he must gain enough ground to destroy the Chickamauga bridges. He broke off the end of their last goods van and dropped it and various sleepers behind him, and this sufficiently checked the pursuit to enable him on two occasions to take in wood and water. More than once his party almost succeeded in lifting a rail, but each time Fuller got within rifle range before the work was completed. Through it all it rained, a steady even-down deluge. The day before had been clear, with a high wind, and a fire would have been quick to start, but on that Saturday, to burn a bridge would take time and much fuel.

On went the chase, mile after mile, past little forgotten stations and quiet villages, round perilous curves, and over culverts and embankments which had never before known such speed. Hope revived whenever the enemy was lost sight of behind a curve, but whenever the line straightened the smoke appeared again in the distance, and on their ears fell the ominous scream of his whistle. To the men, strung to a desperate tension, every minute seemed an hour. If the Northerners' courage was superb, so also was the pursuit's. Several times Fuller only escaped wreck by a hairbreadth. At one point a rail placed across the track at a curve was not seen until the train was upon it, when, said Fuller, "the engine seemed to bounce altogether off the track, and to alight again on the rails by a miracle." A few of the soldiers lost their nerve and would have given up the chase, but the stubborn resolution of their leader constrained them.

Some of Andrews' party now proposed that they should turn and ambush the enemy, getting into close quarters so that their revolvers would be a match for his guns. This plan would probably have succeeded, but Andrews still hoped to gain sufficient ground to achieve his main purpose; and he feared, too, that the country ahead might have been warned by a telegram sent round to Chattanooga by way of Richmond. He thought his only chance was to stake everything on speed. Close to the town of Dalton he stopped again to cut wires and confuse the track. A Confederate regiment was encamped a hundred yards away, but, assuming that the train was part of the normal traffic, the men scarcely lifted their eyes to look at it. Fuller had written a telegram to Chattanooga and dropped a man with orders to send it. Part of the telegram got through before the wires were cut and created a panic in that town. Meantime, Andrews' supply of fuel was getting very low, and it was clear that unless he could delay the pursuit long enough to take in more, his journey would soon come to an end.

Beyond Dalton the adventurers made their last efforts to take up a rail, but, as they had no tools except an iron bar, the coming of the enemy compelled them to desist. Beyond that was a long tunnel, which they made no attempt to damage. Andrews saw that the situation was getting desperate, and he played his last card.

He increased speed so that he gained some considerable distance. Then the side and end boards of the last goods van were broken up, fuel was piled upon it, and fire brought from the engine. A long covered bridge lay a little ahead, and by the time they reached it the van was fairly on fire. It was uncoupled in the middle of the bridge, and they awaited the issue. If this device was successful there was sufficient steam in their boiler to carry them to the next woodyard.

But the device did not succeed. Before the bridge had caught fire Fuller was upon them. He dashed right through the smoke and drove the burning car before him to the next side track.

Left with very little fuel and with no obstructions to drop on the track, the position of the adventurers was now hopeless. In a few minutes their engine would come to a standstill. Their only chance was to leave it and escape. The wisest plan would probably have been to desert the train in a body, move northward through the mountains by tracks which could not be followed by cavalry, and where there were no telegraphs. But Andrews thought that they should separate. He ordered the men to jump from the engine one by one and disperse in the woods. So ended in failure a most gallant enterprise.

Melancholy is the conclusion of the tale. Ignorant of the country and far from their friends, the fugitives were easily hunted down. Several were captured the same day, and all but two within the week. As the adventurers had been in civil dress inside the enemy's lines they were regarded as spies, court-martialed, and Andrews and seven others condemned and executed. The advance of the Northern forces prevented the trial of the rest, and of the remainder, eight succeeded in making their escape from Atlanta in broad daylight, and ultimately reaching the North. The others, who also made the attempt, were recaptured and held captive till March 1863, when they were exchanged for Confederate prisoners.

I know of few stories where the enterprise was at once so audacious and so feasible, where success turned upon such an infinity of delicate chances, and where it was missed by so slender a margin.

III

THE ESCAPE OF KING CHARLES AFTER WORCESTER

Cromwell.

On Wednesday, the 3rd of September 1651, the army which had marched from Scotland to set King Charles upon the throne was utterly defeated by Cromwell at Worcester. The fight began at one o'clock and lasted [illegible] after the main action being lost because of the [illegible]. Many of the chief Royalists, like the Duke of Hamilton, fell on the field. When the issue was clear, Charles, accompanied by the Duke of Buckingham, Lords Derby, Lauderdale, Lord Wilmot, and others, entered the city by Sidbury Gate. There an ammunition wagon had been overturned and this gave check for a moment to the pursuit. In Friars Street the King threw off his armour and was given a fresh horse, and the whole party galloped through the streets and out at St. Martin's Gate. Charles was wearing the laced coat of the Cavalier, a linen doublet, grey breeches, and buff gloves with blue silk bands and silver lace. The little party, dusty and begrimed with battle, galloped to the Barbon Bridge, a mile north of the city, where they halted for a moment to plan their journey.

The nearest and most obvious refuge was Wales,

III

THE ESCAPE OF KING CHARLES AFTER WORCESTER

I

On Wednesday, the third day of September 1651, the army which had marched from Scotland to set King Charles upon the throne was utterly defeated by Cromwell at Worcester. The battle began at one o'clock and lasted during the autumn afternoon, the main action being fought east of the city. Many of the chief Royalists, like the Duke of Hamilton, fell on the field. When the issue was clear, Charles, accompanied by the Duke of Buckingham, Lord Derby, Lord Shrewsbury, Lord Wilmot, and others, entered the city by Sidbury Gate. There an ammunition wagon had been overturned, and this gave check for a moment to the pursuit. In Friars Street the King threw off his armour and was given a fresh horse, and the whole party galloped through the streets and out at St. Martin's Gate. Charles was wearing the laced coat of the Cavalier, a linen doublet, grey breeches, and buff gloves with blue silk bands and silver lace. The little party, dusty and begrimed with battle, galloped to the Barbon Bridge, a mile north of the city, where they halted for a moment to plan their journey.

The nearest and most obvious refuge was Wales,

where the country people were Royalist, and where, in the mountains, Cromwell's troopers might well be defied. But there was no chance of crossing the Severn in that neighbourhood, so it was decided to ride north into Shropshire. Colonel Careless offered to act as rearguard and stave off the pursuit, and Mr. Charles Giffard, of the ancient family of the Giffards of Chillington, who knew the forest country of the Staffordshire and Shropshire borders, undertook the business of guide. There was a place called Boscobel, an old hunting lodge among the woods, where Lord Derby had already been concealed a few weeks before, so Giffard and a servant called Francis Yates (who was afterwards captured by the Cromwellians and executed) led the little band through the twilight meadows.

They passed the town of Kidderminster on their left, where, at the moment, Mr. Richard Baxter, the Presbyterian divine, was watching from an upper window in the market-place the defeated Royalists galloping through and a small party of Cromwellian soldiers firing wildly at the fugitives. The main road was no place for the King when the bulk of the Scottish horse was fleeing northward by that way, so he turned through Stourbridge and halted two miles farther on at a wayside inn to drink a glass of ale and eat a crust of bread. After that they passed through the boundaries of the old Brewood Forest, and at about four o'clock on the morning of Thursday, 4th September, arrived at the ancient half-timbered manor of Whiteladies, belonging to the family of Giffard. A certain George Penderel was in charge as bailiff, and at the sight of the party he stuck his head out of the window and asked for news of the battle. The door was flung open, and the King rode his horse into the hall. Charles was taken into the inner parlour, and George's brothers, William and Richard Penderel, were sent for. Richard was bidden fetch his best clothes, which were breeches of coarse green cloth and a leathern doublet. Charles changed into them, his hair was shorn, and he was now no more the Cavalier, but a countryman of the name of Will Jones, armed with a woodbill.

It would have been fatal for the party to have remained together, so his companions galloped off in the direction of Newport, where most of them were taken prisoner. Lord Derby was captured and afterwards beheaded; Giffard also was taken, but he managed to escape, as did Talbot and Buckingham. Charles was led by Richard Penderel into a wood at the back of the house called Spring Coppice, where he had to make himself as comfortable as might be under the trees.

All that day, Thursday, 4th September, it rained incessantly. Richard Penderel brought him food and blankets, and Charles, worn out with want of sleep, dozed till the dusk of the evening. Then Penderel aroused him and bade him be going. His proposal was to guide him south-west to Madeley, where there seemed a chance of crossing the Severn into Wales. Madeley lay only nine miles to the south-west, a pleasant walk among woods and meadows; but on that autumn night, with the rain falling in bucketfuls and every field a bog, it was a dismal journey for a young man stiff from lying all day in the woods, and stayed by no better meal than eggs and milk. Charles was a hearty trencherman, and had not trained his body to put up with short commons. However, he was given some bacon and eggs before he started.

The Penderels were Catholics, and men of that faith were accustomed in those days to secret goings and desperate shifts, and, since all were half-outlawed, there was a freemasonry between them. Therefore Richard proposed to take the King to a Catholic friend of his, Mr. Francis Wolfe, on the Severn bank, who might conceal him and pass him across the river into

Wales. That journey in the rain remained in the King's mind as a time of peculiar hardships, though there seems no particular difficulty in an active young man walking nine miles at leisure in the darkness. In after years Charles was a famous walker, and used to tire out all his courtiers both by his pace and endurance. But on this occasion he appears to have been footsore and unnerved. When they had gone a mile they had to pass a water-mill and cross a little river by a wooden bridge. The miller came out and asked them their errand; whereupon Penderel took alarm and splashed through the water, followed by his King. After that Charles almost gave up. Lord Clarendon, to whom he told the story, says that "he many times cast himself upon the ground with a desperate and obstinate resolution to rest there till the morning that he might shift with less torment, what hazard so ever he ran. But his stout guide still prevailed with him to make a new attempt, sometimes promising that the way should be better and sometimes assuring him that he had but little farther to go." Charles was desperately footsore. Perhaps the country shoes of "Will Jones" did not fit him.

In the small hours they arrived at Mr. Wolfe's house. Charles waited "under a hedge by a great tree" while Richard Penderel went forward to meet his friend. He was greeted with bad news. Every ford, every bridge, and every ferry on the Severn was guarded by the Cromwellians, who were perfectly aware that the King would make for Wales. Wolfe had "priests' holes" in his house, but he did not dare to hide the King there, for they had already been discovered by the soldiers; so Charles was concealed among the hay in the barn, where he lay during the day of Friday the 5th. There was nothing for it but to take refuge at Boscobel, the hiding-place originally arranged. That night, after borrowing a few shillings from Wolfe, the King and Richard set off eastward again, guided

Penderel took alarm and splashed through the water, followed by his King.

See page 42.

for the first part of the road by Mr. Wolfe's maid. At Whiteladies they heard that Colonel Careless, who was acting as rearguard, had safely reached the Boscobel neighbourhood, and that Lord Wilmot was at Moseley, in Staffordshire, nine or ten miles to the east. All the country was thick woodland interspersed with heaths, and few safer hiding-places could be found in England.

Charles was now in better form. The Penderels had stripped off his stockings, washed his feet and anointed the blisters. His disguise was also perfected, for his face and hands had been dyed with juice, and he made gallant efforts to imitate the clumsy gait of a yokel. But his disguise can never have been very perfect. The harsh features, the curious curl of the lips, the saturnine dark eyes, and above all the figure and the speech, were not such as are commonly found among mid-England peasantry.

Penderel did not dare take him into the house, so he took refuge in the wood, where he was presently joined by Colonel Careless. On the coast being reported clear, the King spent the night in one of the priests' holes in the old manor, an uncomfortable dormitory, which had, however, a gallery adjoining it, where he took walking exercise and surveyed the road from Tong to Brewood. Saturday the 6th was a fine day, and the King spent some time sitting in an arbour in the garden. He was presently induced by Colonel Careless to seek a safer retreat in an oak tree in the wood. A little platform was made in the upper branches, pillows were brought from the house, and there Careless and the King spent the day. The Royal Oak is famous in Stuart history, and this particular tree has long since been hacked to pieces to make keepsakes for the faithful. But it is by no means certain that Charles was in particular danger during the day that he slept in it, or that any Roundhead trooper rode below the branches and "hummed a surly hymn." Careless had the worst part of the business, for the King rested his head in his lap and the honest soldier's arm went to sleep. "This," in the words of the *Miraculum Basilicon*, "caused such a stupor or numbness in the part, that he had scarcely strength left in it any longer to support His Majesty from falling off the tree, neither durst he by reason of the nearness of the enemy speak so loud as to awake him; nevertheless, to avoid both the danger of the fall and surprise together, he was (though unwillingly) constrained to practise so much incivility as to pinch His Majesty, to the end he might awake him to prevent his present danger."

When the dusk came the two descended and went into the manor-house. There they were met by the news that the enemy cordon was closing round, and that £1,000 reward had been put upon the King's head. Charles, however, was in no way dismayed, and demanded a loin of mutton. William Penderel accordingly fetched one of his master's sheep, which Careless stabbed and cut up with his dagger. The King made Scotch collops of a hind-quarter, which the Colonel fried in a pan, and the two had a hearty meal.

The King slept that night in the house in a "priest's hole," and next day resolved to join Lord Wilmot at Moseley. He found, however, that his feet were still so tender that walking was impossible, so an old mill horse that had carried provisions in the campaign was found for him. Mounted on this beast, attended by Careless and the Penderels, the King set out in the dusk of the Sunday evening. At Moseley he found Lord Wilmot, and since Moseley was a safer place than Boscobel, the King spent a peaceful night in the house. There, too, was a priest, Father John Huddleston, and not far off was Colonel Lane, both devoted Royalists. There he said farewell to his staunch friends, the Penderels. The King, we are told, spent the evening by the fire while Father Huddlestone attended to his unfortunate feet. Charles had stuffed his stockings with paper, but the precaution had not saved him from further galls and sores. He was given new worsted stockings and clean linen and slippers, and was so much cheered thereby that he declared he was now fit for a new march, and that "if it should ever please God to bless him with ten or twelve thousand loyal and resolute men, he doubted not to drive these traitors out of his kingdom."

We have this description of Charles on his arrival at Moseley: "He had on his head a long white steeple-crowned hat, without any other lining than grease, both sides of the brim so doubled with handling that they looked like two spouts; a leather doublet full of holes, and half black with grease above the sleeves, collar, and waist; an old green woodreve's coat, threadbare and patched in most places, with a pair of breeches of the same cloth and in the same condition, the flaps hanging down loose to the middle of his legs; hose and shoes of different parishes; the hose were grey, much darned and clouted, especially about the knees, under which he had a pair of flannel riding-stockings of his own with the tops cut off. His shoes had been cobbled with leather patches both on the soles and the seams, and the upper-leathers so cut and slashed, to adapt them to his feet, that they could no longer defend him either from water or dirt. This exotic and deformed dress, added to his short hair by the ears, his face coloured brown with walnut leaves, and a rough crooked thorn stick in his hand, had so metamorphosed him, he became scarcely discernible who he was, even to those that had been before acquainted with his person."

Next day, Monday, the 8th, it was given out that Father Huddleston had a Cavalier friend lying privately in the house, and all the servants were sent away on errands except the cook, who was a Catholic. Watch was kept at the different windows in case of any roving party of soldiers. The King spent the day largely in sleeping and discussing the future, while messages were sent to loyal neighbouring squires to find out the lie of the land. He saw a sad sight from the windows—many starving Royalist soldiers limping past the door, munching cabbage stalks and corn plucked from the fields. However, he heard one piece of news of some importance. Colonel Lane, who lived five miles off at Bentley, had a sister, Miss Jane, who had procured a pass from the Governor of Stafford for herself and her servant to go to Bristol, and it was thought that if the King passed as her servant he might thereby get clear of the country. It was accordingly arranged that on the Tuesday night Lord Wilmot's horses should fetch the King to Bentley, as the first stage of his journey to the Bristol Channel.

On the Tuesday afternoon, however, the plan all but miscarried. A party of soldiers arrived to search Moseley, and the King was hurriedly hustled into one of the "priest's holes." The place is still pointed out—a stuffy little nook behind the panelling, through which liquid food used to be conveyed to the unfortunate occupant by means of a quill through a chink in the beams. The soldiers made a great row, and questioned the owner, Mr. Whitgreave, with a musket cocked at his breast, but in the end departed. When dusk fell Colonel Lane's horses arrived, and Charles set out and arrived safely at Bentley. There Colonel Lane gave him, in place of Will Jones's unspeakable clothes, a good suit and cloak of country grey, like a farmer's son, and put £20 in his pocket for the expenses of the journey.

II

The King is now no longer an aimless wanderer among the Staffordshire woods. A plan of campaign had been evolved, and the fugitive in a reasonable disguise is making for the sea. He arrived at Bentley about midnight on 9th September. The party that set out on the 10th consisted of Miss Jane Lane, her cousin, Mrs. Petre, Mr. Petre, that cousin's husband, and a certain Cornet Henry Lassels, also a kinsman. The Petres were bound for their house at Horton, in Buckinghamshire, and proposed to go only as far as Stratford-on-Avon. Charles rode in front as Miss Jane's servant. The route lay by Bromsgrove and Stratford-on-Avon, then through Cotswold to Cirencester, and thence to Bristol.

It was a bold enterprise, for the natural route of flight after Worcester would be down the Severn valley to the sea. Cromwell's troopers were in every parish, and a large part of the population, knowing of the King's escape and the reward for his capture, were on the watch for any suspicious stranger. The first stop was at the village of Bromsgrove, where the King's horse cast a shoe. In the smithy Charles, in his character of servant, asked the smith the news. "Precious little," was the answer, "except that Cromwell has routed the Scots. He has slain or captured most of them, but I hear the King has made his escape." "Perhaps," said Charles, "the King has gone by by-ways back into Scotland." "No," said the smith, "there is not much luck for him that way. He is lurking secretly somewhere in these parts, and I wish I knew where he were, for then I would be the richer by a thousand pounds."

Nothing more happened till they came near Stratford, riding as hard as they could by secluded by-ways. Their plan was to ford the Avon about a mile below the town; but when they drew near the river they observed soldiers' horses feeding in the meadows and many troopers lying upon the ground. This sight made them turn to their left so as to enter Stratford another way. But at the bridge there they ran full into the same troop of soldiers. The troop opened right and left to let them pass, and returned the civil salute which the little party gave them.

They were now among the foothills of Cotswold, and before evening reached the straggling village of Long Marston, a place famous for its morrice dancing. In the village there was a certain Mr. John Tomes, and in his house the travellers found lodging. The King, passing as a servant, found his way to the kitchen, where, like an earlier monarch of England, he was scolded by the cook because he had no notion how to wind up a roasting-jack. The said jack is still in existence, and is to be seen in the village. Meantime Lord Wilmot and Colonel Lane were following behind, and the latter turned off towards London, in order to arrange the final details of a pass for "Will Jackson," which was the name the King had now adopted.

On Thursday morning, 11th September, the travellers began the ascent into the Cotswold moors. In that empty country of sheep-walks there was less risk of detection, and accordingly good speed was made by Stow-on-the-Wold and along the old Roman Fosse Way to Northleach and so to Cirencester, where they arrived in the evening, after a ride of thirty-six miles. Near the market-place stood the "Crown Inn," an inconspicuous hostelry, and the travellers, professing great fatigue, went immediately to bed. In one chamber a good bed was prepared for Mr. Lassels and a truckle bed for Will Jackson; but as soon as the door was closed the King went to sleep in the good bed and the Cornet on the pallet.

Next day, Friday, 12th September, the party rode twenty-two miles south-west to Chipping Sodbury, probably escorted for part of the way by Captain Matthew Huntley, an old soldier of Prince Rupert's, who lived in these parts. They entered the city of Bristol by Lawford's Gate, rode through the streets, crossed the Avon by a ferry, and kept the left bank of the river to the village of Abbots Leigh, three miles west of Bristol. Abbots Leigh, which stands high up on the Downs, was an old Elizabethan house belonging to the family of Norton. There the King was in safe quarters. Miss Jane ordered a bed to be made for him in a private room, and gave out that he was the son of one of her father's tenants and was sick of an ague. A neighbouring Royalist country gentleman, Dr. Gorge, was called in to prescribe. Seeing that the party had come from the north, Gorge asked the King for news of battle. When Charles faltered in his answer the doctor accused him of being a Roundhead. The King denied the charge, and was there and then compelled to prove his politics by drinking a glass of wine to his own health.

For four days Charles pretended to be sick, and sat in the chimney corner, while Miss Jane complained to heaven of the feebleness of her servant. "That wretched boy will never be good for anything again," she told all and sundry. One day the King, while eating his bread and cheese in the buttery, fell into talk with a man who had been at Worcester, and asked him if he had ever seen the King. "Twenty times," was the answer. "What kind of a fellow is he?" The man looked at Charles steadfastly. "He is," he said, "four fingers' breadth taller than you." At that moment Mrs. Norton passed and Charles took off his hat to her. The butler, who had never seen him uncovered, saw something in his face which he remembered. He took occasion a little later, when they were alone, to ask if he were not the King. Charles confessed that he was, and the butler—one John Pope, who had been once a falconer of Sir Thomas Jermyn, and afterwards a Royalist soldier—swore secrecy and fealty. Another person was now in the plot, and Pope was used as a messenger to Bristol to find out what ships were sailing. But the news was bad. No vessel could be obtained there, and since it was clear that the King could not stay on at Abbots Leigh, it was resolved to seek the hospitality of Colonel Francis Wyndham, who lived at Trent on the Dorsetshire borders. The aim was to reach the south coast, where a smack might be hired to carry him into France.

Lord Wilmot, who had arrived at Abbots Leigh soon after the King, was sent off to Trent to inquire whether the Wyndhams would hide His Majesty. He brought back a reply that Wyndham "thought himself extremely happy that amongst so many noble and loyal subjects he should be reckoned chiefly worthy of that honour, and that he was ready not only to venture his life, family, and estate, but even to sacrifice all to His Majesty's service." There was some difficulty about the departure of Miss Jane. The lady at Abbots Leigh had just had a child and implored her friend not to leave her. An imaginary letter was accordingly fabricated, purporting to be from Miss Jane's father, demanding her immediate return on the ground of his sudden and dangerous illness.

On the 16th Miss Jane, Lassels, and Charles set out for Dorsetshire, going first towards Bristol as if they were returning to Bentley. Presently they turned the horses' heads south towards Castle Cary, where they were to sleep that night. The manor there was occupied by Lord Hertford's steward, one Edward Kirton, who had been advised by Lord Wilmot to look out for the travellers. Next day a ride of ten miles brought the party to Trent, where Colonel Francis Wyndham and his wife, Lady Anne, were waiting to receive them. The Wyndhams, as if taking an evening walk, met their guests before the house was reached. Miss Jane and Lassels were publicly received as relations, but Charles was brought secretly into the old house.

Next morning the King parted with Miss Jane,

who had been the Flora Macdonald of his Odyssey. She lived thirty-eight years after that eventful journey, marrying Sir Clement Fisher of Packington, a Warwickshire squire. She became a famous toast to Royalists, and the many portraits extant reveal a lady of pleasing aspect, with a certain resolution and vigour in her air. The King gave her many gifts, the House of Lords presented her with jewels, and she and all her relations had royal pensions. Her brother, Colonel Lane, was offered but declined a peerage. The family were granted an augmentation to their coat of arms, and the motto "Garde le Roi" to commemorate their achievement.

Trent was a good hiding-place and within reasonable distance of the coast, so that negotiations could be entered upon for a vessel to carry His Majesty to France. There Charles stayed several days, living in a set of four rooms, which are still unaltered. One day the bells of the neighbouring church rang out a peal, and the King sent to inquire the reason for the rejoicing. He was told that one of Cromwell's troopers was in the village, who announced that he had killed Charles, and was even then wearing his buff coat, and that the villagers, being mostly Puritans, were celebrating the joyful news.

Meanwhile Colonel Wyndham was hunting high and low for a ship. He consulted his neighbour, Colonel Strangways of Melbury, the ancestor of the Ilchester family; and a certain William Ellesdon, a merchant of Lyme Regis, was named as a likely person to procure a vessel, since he had already assisted Lord Berkeley to escape. Ellesdon suggested a tenant of his, one Stephen Limbry of Charmouth, the master of a coasting vessel, and for £60 the latter agreed to carry Lord Wilmot and his servant to France. Limbry was to have his long boat ready at Charmouth on the night of the 22nd.

The next thing was to get rooms at Charmouth for

that night, and Wyndham's servant was sent to an inn—" The Queen's Arms "—in that place, with a tale of how he served a worthy nobleman who was deep in love with an orphan maid and was resolved to steal her by night. The romantic hostess believed the story, and agreed to give them rooms and keep her tongue quiet. Accordingly Charles set out on the morning of 22nd September from Trent, riding pillion with a certain Miss Juliana Coningsby, Colonel Wyndham's pretty cousin, who was to play the part of the runaway heroine. Colonel Wyndham went as a guide, and Lord Wilmot and his servant followed behind. On the way to Charmouth they met Ellesdon, who learned for the first time that the King was the fugitive. Charles made the merchant a present of a gold coin in which he had bored a hole to wile away the dreary hours of his hiding in Trent In the afternoon the little party rode down the steep hill into Charmouth, arriving at the inn of the romantic landlady, while Ellesdon went to hunt up Limbry, the seaman.

It was an anxious moment, for, as luck would have it, it was market day at Lyme and the inn was crowded. Lord Wilmot and Miss Coningsby had to live up to the part of runaway lovers—a part in which Charles would probably have shown more zeal than discretion.

Midnight came, but there was no sign of Limbry. Wyndham and his servant were out all night on the quest, but at dawn they returned to report failure. The first idea was that the man must have got drunk at the market ; but later the true story came out. Limbry had gone home to get clean clothes for the voyage. But that day a proclamation had been made in the town declaring it death for any person to aid or conceal the King, and promising £1,000 reward for his apprehension. His wife, knowing her husband's practices in the past, accordingly locked him in his room, and when he would have broken out raised racket enough to alarm the neighbourhood. The prudent man made a virtue of necessity and submitted.

Here was a pretty kettle of fish. Charles could not stay at Charmouth, and it was arranged that he and Miss Coningsby and Wyndham should ride on to Bridport, while Lord Wilmot and his servant should remain behind for an explanation with Ellesdon. A rendezvous was to be made at the "George Inn" at Bridport. Off went the King, while Lord Wilmot's horse went to the smithy to be shod. The smith, who was a stout Cromwellian, began to ask questions. Whence came these nails if the gentlemen had ridden from Exeter, for these nails were assuredly put in in the North? The ostler in charge of the horse added that the saddles had not been taken off in the night time, and that the gentlemen, though travellers, sat up all night. Clearly they were people of quality fleeing from the Worcester fight, and probably the King was among them. The ostler saw a chance of making his fortune, and marched off to the parsonage to consult the parson, one Wesley, the great grandfather of the famous John. It is interesting to note that just as Lord Macaulay's great grandfather did his best to prevent Prince Charlie's escape, so John Wesley's great-grandfather came athwart that of King Charles.

But Mr. Wesley was busy at his morning devotions and would not move till they were ended. On hearing the tale he accompanied the ostler to the inn, where, being apparently a humorist, he thus accosted the landlady: "Charles Stuart lay last night at your house and kissed you at his departure, so that now you can't but be a maid of honour." "If I thought it was the King, as you say it was," was the answer, "I would think the better of my lips all the days of my life. Out of my house, Mr. Parson." So Mr. Parson went to the nearest commanding officer and got a troop of horse together, who followed what they believed to be the track of the fugitives along the London road.

Meantime Charles had arrived at Bridport. The town was packed with soldiers who had mustered there for an expedition against the Isle of Jersey. It was no easy matter to get lodgings at the "George"; but there he must go, for it was the rendezvous appointed with Lord Wilmot. A private room was found with some difficulty, while the King attended to the horses in the yard. There he met a drunken ostler who claimed to have known him in Exeter; the King played up to this part and the two made merry together. A hurried dinner was eaten, for there was no time to linger, and as soon as Lord Wilmot had joined them they pushed on along the London road. A quarter of an hour after they left the "George" the local authorities arrived to search it (the news of the Royalists' presence having come from Charmouth), and more soldiers started in pursuit. Luckily the King's party resolved to go back to Trent, and had just turned off the high road when they saw the pursuit dash past in the direction of Dorchester.

After that the travellers seemed to have lost their way, but in the evening they found themselves in the village of Broad Windsor, close to Trent. In the inn there Colonel Wyndham recognized in the landlord a former servant and a staunch Royalist, and there they slept the night. It was a narrow lodging and much congested with forty soldiers, who were marching to the south coast on the Jersey expedition. No untoward event, however, happened, and next morning the King got back to his old quarters in Trent. There he lay secure while his pursuers were laying hands upon every handsome young lady for forty miles round, under the belief that it was their monarch in disguise. The honest folk of Charmouth and Bridport seem to have seen the King in Miss Julia Coningsby, and, indeed, this belief in Charles's female disguise was almost universal. There was another rumour in London that, wearing a red periwig, he had actually got a post as servant to an officer of Cromwell's army; and still another, published on 29th September, that he was safe in Scotland with Lord Balcarres.

III

The problem of escape had now become exceedingly difficult. It was impossible to stay on the coast, which was strictly watched, and was, moreover, all in a bustle with the Jersey expedition. But the coast was the only hope, and therefore it must be again visited. The only chance was to make a cast inland and try for the shore at another point. While at Trent, Colonel Wyndham's brother-in-law, Mr. Edward Hyde, came to dine, and mentioned that on the previous day at Salisbury he had seen Colonel Robert Phelips of Montacute, who could probably get them a vessel in one of the southern ports. Lord Wilmot was accordingly sent off next morning to Salisbury to find Colonel Phelips and devise a plan.

Phelips willingly undertook the service and went off to Southampton to look for a ship. He thought he had found one; but it turned out that the bark was pressed to carry provisions to Admiral Blake's fleet, then lying before Jersey. He returned to Salisbury, and decided to get the assistance of a certain Colonel Gounter who lived near Chichester. It was agreed that Charles should be brought to Heale House, near Salisbury, the residence of a widow, a Mrs. Hyde, and there, on Monday, 6th October, accompanied by Miss Juliana Coningsby, the King duly arrived from Trent. At Heale Miss Juliana left him, having faithfully played her romantic part. To dinner came Dr. Hinchman, afterwards Bishop of Salisbury, and next day the King behaved like an ordinary tourist, riding out to see the sights, especially Stonehenge. Meanwhile Lord Wilmot was scouring the country for a man who would hire him a boat, and he and Colonel Gounter thought their likeliest chance was with a certain Captain Nicholas Tattersal, the master of a small coal brig, the *Surprise*, at Brighton. Tattersal, however, had just started for Chichester; but a message reached him at Shoreham, and on Saturday, 11th October, there was a meeting, when, for £60, the captain agreed to carry over to France Colonel Gounter's two friends, who were said to be anxious to leave the country because of their part in a fatal duel.

It was now necessary to get the King from Heale to the Sussex coast. At two o'clock on the Monday morning Charles rode out of Heale by the back way with Colonel Phelips, and took the road for Hampshire. After they had covered about fifteen miles they were joined by Colonel Gounter and Lord Wilmot, who, by previous arrangement, had been coursing hares on the Downs. They spent the night in a house at Hambledon among the pleasant hills of the Forest of Bere, where they parted with Phelips. Colonel Gounter was now in charge, and on Tuesday, the 14th, their way lay through the county of Sussex. Charles's disguise must have been fairly complete, for he seems usually to have been taken for a Parliamentarian, since William Penderel's scissors had left him with very little hair. He took pains to keep up the character, for when an innkeeper used an oath, he flung up his hands and drawled, "Oh, dear brother, that is a 'scape.' Swear not, I beseech thee." He was clad in a short coat and breeches of sad-coloured cloth, with a black hat, and, according to one narrative, cut a figure like "the minor sort of country gentleman."

This last day's ride was in many ways the most hazardous of all. As they neared Arundel Castle they suddenly encountered the Governor setting out to hunt with some of his men. Crossing the Arun at Houghton Bridge, they had beer at a poor alehouse and lunched off two neat's tongues, which Colonel Gounter had brought with him. Then they passed through the pretty village of Bramber, which, as it happened, was full of Cromwellian soldiers who had stopped for refreshment. When they had left the village behind them they heard a clattering at their back and saw the whole troop riding as if in pursuit. The soldiers, however, galloped past them without stopping, and at the next village, Beeding, where Colonel Gounter had arranged a meal for the King, they did not dare to halt for fear of the same soldiers. Nine miles more over the Downs and they reached the obscure little fishing village of Brighthelmstone, which was all that then existed of Brighton, and halted at the "George Inn," where they ordered supper.

The place was happily empty, and there Lord Wilmot joined them. That last meal was a merry one, and Charles was especially cheerful, for he saw his long suspense approaching its end. He had borne the strain with admirable fortitude and good-humour, and whatever may be said of his qualities as a king on the throne, he was certainly an excellent king of adventure. The landlord, one Smith, who had formerly been in the Royal Guards, waited on the table at supper and apparently recognized His Majesty, for he kissed his hand and said, "It shall not be said that I have not kissed the best man's hand in England. God bless you! I do not doubt but, before I die, to be a lord and my wife a lady." Tattersal, the shipmaster, also joined them, and they sat drinking and smoking until 10 p.m., when it was time to start.

Horses were brought by the back way to the beach, and the party rode along the coast to Shoreham Creek. There lay the coal brig, the *Surprise*, and Charles and Lord Wilmot got into her by way of her ladder and lay down in the little cabin till the tide turned, after bidding adieu to Colonel Gounter. The honest Colonel waited upon the shore with the horses for some hours, lest some accident should drive the party ashore again.

It was between seven and eight o'clock in the morning of Wednesday, 15th October, before the boat sailed, making apparently for the Isle of Wight, the captain having given out that he was bound for Poole with a cargo of sea coal. At five o'clock that evening they changed direction, and with a favourable north wind set out for the French coast. The King amused himself on deck by directing the course, for he knew something of navigation. Next morning the coast of France was sighted, but a change in the wind and the falling tide compelled them to anchor two miles off Fécamp. Charles and Wilmot rowed ashore in the cock-boat. Thereafter the wind turned again, and enabled Tattersal to proceed to Poole without any one being aware that he had paid a visit to France.

After the Restoration the little coal boat was ornamented and enlarged and moored in the Thames at Whitehall as a show for Londoners. She now bore the name of the *Royal Escape*, and was entered as a fifth-rater in the Royal Navy.

Wilmot, the loyal and resourceful companion, did not live to see the Restoration, for he died in the autumn of 1657, after he had been created Earl of Rochester. Nine years after the events recorded in this tale, on the 25th May, in bright weather, Charles landed at Dover at the summons of his countrymen, as the restored King of England. He was met by the Mayor and presented with a Bible, which, he observed, was the thing he most valued in the world. So began a reign which was scarcely worthy of its spirited prelude. In one matter, indeed, the King was beyond criticism. No one of the people, gentle or simple, who had assisted him in that wild flight from Worcester died unrewarded. Until the end of his days Charles cherished tenderly the memory of the weeks when he had been an outlaw with a price on his head, and king, like Robin Hood, only of the greenwood.

Charles II.

IV

FROM PRETORIA TO THE SEA

I

On November 15, 1899, Lieutenant-General Sir Aylmer Haldane, who in the Great War commanded the VI. Corps, was thirty-seven years of age and a captain in the Gordon Highlanders. Mr. Winston Churchill, who was afterwards to hold most offices in the British Cabinet, was then twenty-five, and was acting as correspondent for the *Morning Post* on the Natal front. He had already seen service with his regiment, the 4th Hussars, on the Indian frontier, and in other capacities in Cuba and on the Nile. The South African War had just begun, and so far had gone badly for Britain. Sir George White was cut off in Ladysmith; but Sir Redvers Buller had landed in Natal, and it was believed that he would soon advance to an easy victory.

The South African War, as we all know, was entered upon light-heartedly and with very scanty fore-knowledge of the problems to be faced. Much of the British equipment was amateurish; but the palm for amateurishness must be given to the armoured train which plied its trade in the neighbourhood of Estcourt. It was not much better than a death-trap. It was made up of an engine, five wagons, and an ancient 7-pounder muzzle-loading gun. Its purpose was reconnaissance; but it was a very noisy and conspicuous scout, as it wheezed up and down the line, belching clouds of smoke and steam.

On the morning of 15th November it set out to reconnoitre towards Chieveley, carrying on board 120 men, made up of a small civilian break-down gang, part of a company of the Dublin Fusiliers, and a company of the Durban Light Infantry Volunteers. Captain Haldane was in command, and Mr. Churchill, in his capacity as a war correspondent, went with him. When they reached Chieveley, Boer horsemen were observed, and the train was ordered back to Frere. But before it reached Frere it was discovered that a hill commanding the whole line at a distance of 600 yards was occupied by the enemy.

The driver put on full steam and tried to run the gauntlet; but a big stone had been placed on the line at the foot of a steep gradient, and into this the train crashed. The engine, which was in the centre of the train, was not derailed, and a gallant attempt was made to clear the wreckage of the foremost trucks and push through. For more than an hour, under heavy shell-fire from the enemy's field guns, and a constant hail of rifle bullets, the crew of the train laboured to clear the obstruction. But the couplings of the trucks broke, and though the engine, laden with wounded, managed to continue its journey, the position of the rest of the crew was hopeless, and they were compelled to surrender. The Boers behaved with conspicuous humanity, and the little company of prisoners were soon jogging slowly northward towards Pretoria.

The capital of the then South African Republic was a little town planned in orderly parallelograms lying in a cup among rocky hills. From it three railways radiated—one to Pietersburg and the north, one to Johannesburg in the south-west, and one running eastward to Portuguese territory and the sea at Delagoa Bay. The British privates and non-commissioned officers were sent to a camp at the racecourse on the outskirts of the town, while the officers were taken to the Staats Model School, a building almost in the centre of Pretoria. At first Mr. Churchill was sent with the men, but he was presently brought back and added to the officers. He bore a name which was better known than liked in the Transvaal at the time, and his presence as a prisoner was a considerable satisfaction to his captors.

The Staats Model School was a single-storied red brick building with a slated veranda, and consisted of twelve class-rooms, a large lecture-hall, and a gymnasium. The playground in which it stood was about 120 yards square, and in it there were tents for the guards, the cookhouse, and a bathing-shed. On two sides it was surrounded by an iron grill, and on the other two by a corrugated iron fence some 10 feet high. Before the prisoners from the armoured train arrived there were already sixty British officers there, captured in the early Natal fighting. For guard there were twenty-seven men and three corporals of the South African Republic Police (known locally as "Zarps"). These furnished nine sentries in reliefs of four hours; they stood 50 yards apart, well armed with revolvers and rifles. In every street of Pretoria, too, were posted special armed constables.

To be taken prisoner thus early, in what was believed to be a triumphant war, was a bitter pill for British officers to swallow, and it was not easier for the restless, energetic spirit of Mr. Churchill. As soon as the captives arrived they began to make plans for escape. None of them were on parole, and at first sight it looked a comparatively easy task. It would not be hard to scale the flimsy outer defences of the Staats Model School, but the trouble lay in the guards. It was found impossible to bribe them, for, as Mr. Churchill has observed in his book, the presence of so many millionaires in the country had raised the tariff too high for any ordinary purse. Another difficulty was where to go to. It was no good attempting to reach Natal or Cape Colony, for that meant going through Boer armies. The best chance lay eastward in the direction of Portuguese territory, but that involved a journey of 300 miles through an unknown country. The one hope was the Delagoa Bay line, for where there is a railway there are always chances of transport for a bold man.

Captain Haldane's mind turned to tunnelling, and he discovered in an old cupboard several screwdrivers and wire-cutters, which he managed to secrete. Mr. Churchill had a more audacious plan. He had observed that the sentries on the side of the quadrangle remote from the road were at certain times, as they walked on their beats, unable to see the top of a few yards of the boundary wall. There were brilliant electric lights in the middle of the quadrangle, but the sentries beyond them could not see very well what lay behind. If it were possible to pass the two sentries on that side at the exact moment when both their backs were turned together, the wall might be scaled and the garden of the villa next door reached. Beyond that it was impossible to plan. Mr. Churchill and a friend resolved to make the attempt and to trust to the standing luck of the British Army to get safely out of the town and cover the 280 miles to the Portuguese border. They had a fair amount of money, they would carry some chocolate with them, and they hoped to buy mealies at the native kraals. They knew no Kafir or Dutch, and would have to lie hidden by day and move only in the darkness.

II

The enterprise was fixed for the night of 11th December, and was to be attempted at seven o'clock when the bell rang for dinner. The two spent a nervous

Then another man joined the first, lit a cigar, and the two walked off together.

See page 66.

afternoon; but when the bell rang it was seen that the thing was hopeless. The sentries did not walk about, and one stood opposite the one climbable part of the wall. "With a most unsatisfactory feeling of relief" the two went to bed. The next evening came and again the dinner-bell rang. Mr. Churchill walked across the quadrangle, and from a corner in one of the offices watched the sentries. After half an hour one suddenly turned and walked up to his comrade and began to talk. The chance had come. Mr. Churchill ran to the wall, pulled himself up, and lay flat on the top while the sentries with their backs turned were talking 15 yards away. Then he dropped into the shrubs of the garden.

It was a night of full moonlight, but there was fair cover in the bushes. The villa to which the garden belonged was 20 yards off, and the undrawn curtains revealed brightly lighted windows with figures moving about. Mr. Churchill had to wait for the arrival of his comrade, and as he waited a man came out of the back door of the villa and walked in his direction across the garden. Ten yards away he stopped and appeared to be watching, while the fugitive remained absolutely still with a thumping heart. Then another man joined the first, lit a cigar, and the two walked off together. Then a cat was pursued by a dog, rushed into the bushes, and collided with the fugitive. The two men stopped, but, reflecting that it was only the cat, passed out of the garden gate into the town.

Mr. Churchill had now been lying there an hour, when he heard a voice from inside the quadrangle say quite loud, "All up." He crawled back to the wall and heard two officers walking up and down talking. One of them mentioned his name. He coughed; one of the officers thereupon began to chatter some kind of nonsense while the other said slowly, "He cannot get out. The sentry suspects. It is all up. Can you get back again?" But to go back was impossible, and though Mr. Churchill had very little hope he determined to have a run for his money. He said loudly and clearly, so that the others heard him, "I shall go on alone."

The first thing was to get out of Pretoria. He had managed during his confinement to acquire a suit of dark clothes, different from the ordinary garments issued to prisoners. To reach the road he must pass a sentry at short range, but he decided that the boldest course was the safest. He got up, walked past the windows of the villa, passed the sentry at less than 50 yards, and, after walking 100 yards and hearing no challenge, knew that he had surmounted the second obstacle.

It was a queer experience to be at large on a bright moonlight night in the heart of the enemy's capital nearly 300 miles from friendly territory, and with a certainty that in an hour or two there would be a hue and cry out against him. He strolled at a leisurely pace down the middle of the streets, humming a tune, past crowds of burghers, till he reached the environs. There he sat down and reflected. His escape would probably not be known till dawn, and he must get some way off before daybreak, for all the neighbouring country would be patrolled. He had £75 in his pocket and four slabs of chocolate, but the compass, map, opium tablets, and meat lozenges were left behind with his unlucky friend. His only chance was the Delagoa Bay Railway. That line, of course, was guarded, and every train would be searched; but among a multitude of black alternatives it gave at least a ray of hope.

Half a mile later he struck the railroad, but he could not be sure whether it was the Pietersburg or the Delagoa Bay line, for it appeared to run north instead of east. He followed it, and soon began to realize the exhilaration of escape. Walking in the cool night under the stars his spirits rose. There were pickets along the line and watchers at every bridge, but he avoided them all by short detours. And as he walked he reflected that if he trusted to his feet to cover the 300 miles he would very soon be captured. He must make better speed, and the only chance for that was a train. Yes, a train must be boarded, and at the earliest opportunity.

When he had walked for two hours he perceived the lights of a station, so he left the track and hid in a ditch 200 yards beyond the buildings. He argued that any train would stop at the station and by the time it reached him would not have got up much speed. After another hour he heard a train whistle and saw the yellow headlights of the engine. It waited five minutes in the station, and then, with a great rumbling, started again. Mr. Churchill flung himself on the trucks, got some sort of handhold, and with a great struggle seated himself on the couplings. It was a goods train, and the trucks were full of empty sacks covered with coal dust, among which he burrowed. He had no notion whether or not he was on the right line, and he was too tired to worry, so he simply fell asleep. He woke before daybreak and realized that he must leave the train ere dawn. So he sat himself again on the couplings, and catching hold of the iron handle at the back of the truck, sprang to the side. The next moment he was sprawling in a ditch, much shaken but not hurt.

He found himself in the middle of a valley surrounded by low hills. Presently the dawn began to break, and to his relief he realized that he had taken the right railway. The line ran straight into the sunrise. He had a long drink from a pool, and resolved to select a hiding-place to lie up for the day. This he found in a patch of wood on the side of a deep ravine, where, in the company of a cynical vulture, he spent the daylight hours. From his eyrie he could see a little tin-roofed town in the west, through which he had passed in the night, and in the immediate neighbourhood farmsteads with clumps of trees. There was a Kafir kraal at the bottom of the hill, and he watched the natives drive the flocks of goats and cows to the pastures. His only food was one slab of chocolate, which produced a violent thirst; but as the water-pool was half a mile away in the open, and men were constantly passing, he dare not risk going for a drink.

His prospects were pretty black when he started again at the first darkness. He had a drink from the pool, and then took to the railway line in hope of getting a second train ride. But no train came, and for six hours in the bright moonlight he walked on, avoiding the Kafirs' huts and the guarded bridges. When he had to make a circuit he fell into bogs, and, as he was in a poor condition from the previous month's imprisonment, he was very soon tired out.

Mr. Churchill published the story of his escape during the war, when it was important not to implicate any friends still in the Transvaal, and so the next part of his journey has never been explicitly told. It appears that he fell in with a Mr. Burnham and a Mr. Howard, officials of a colliery, who gave him valuable assistance, as they were afterwards to assist Captain Haldane. On the fifth day after leaving Pretoria he reached Middelburg, where it was arranged that he should try and board a Delagoa Bay train.

Meantime the hue and cry was out against him. Telegrams describing him at great length were sent along every railway; 3,000 photographs were printed, and warrants were issued for his immediate arrest. Officials of the prison who knew him by sight hurried off to Komati Poort, the frontier station, to examine travellers. It was rumoured that he had escaped disguised as a woman, and again disguised as a policeman; and finally it was reported that he was still in hiding in Pretoria. The Dutch newspapers considered it a sinister fact that just before he escaped he had become a subscriber to the State Library and had borrowed Mill's *On Liberty*!

On the sixth day he found a train to Delagoa Bay standing in a siding, which he boarded. The journey should take not more than thirty-six hours, so the provisions carried were not elaborate, and he had only one bottle of water. He managed to ensconce himself in a truck laden with great sacks of some soft merchandise, and worm his way to the bottom. The heat was stifling, for it was midsummer in the Transvaal, and the floor of the truck was littered with coal dust, which did not add to its amenities.

These last days of the adventure were both anxious and uncomfortable. He scarcely dared to sleep for fear of snoring, and he was in terror that at Komati Poort, the frontier station of the Transvaal, the trucks would be searched. His anxiety there was prolonged, for the train was shunted for eighteen hours on to a siding. Indeed, his truck was actually searched, and the upper tarpaulin was removed, but the police were careless and did not search deep enough.

At length, two and a half days after he left Middelburg, and eight and a half days from Pretoria, the train crawled into Delagoa Bay. Mr. Churchill emerged from his hole in the last stages of dirt, hunger, and weariness. But all troubles were now past. He went first to the British consul, who thought he was a fireman from one of the ships in the harbour, and who welcomed him with enthusiasm when he learned his real name. Clothes were bought; he had a long wash, and at last a civilized meal. That very night, as it happened, a steamer was leaving for Durban, and in case any of the Boer agents at Delagoa Bay should attempt to recapture him, some dozen of the English residents, armed with revolvers, escorted him on board. A few days later Mr. Churchill was back again in Natal with the British Army.

III

We return to Captain Haldane and his friends, who had been meditating escape from the first day of their arrival at the Staats Model School. The difficulty was, of course, the guards, and Mr. Churchill's exploit made the Boer Government redouble its vigilance. It was found impossible to bribe the sentries; a plan for a rising of the prisoners was soon given up; and the scheme of sinking a shaft and then tunnelling to an adjacent kitchen garden proved impracticable, since the diggers very soon struck water. For three miserable months Captain Haldane cogitated in vain, and the best he could do was to get hold of a tourist map of South Africa and study the country east of Pretoria in case some way of escape should present itself. Meantime an incident cheered the prisoners. A man accompanied by a St. Bernard dog took to walking outside the school and signalling by the Morse code with his stick. He was warned off by the guards, but he found another means of communication and sent messages from an adjacent house giving the news of the war.

In the middle of February 1900 there was a rumour that the officers were to be moved to a new building from which escape would be impossible. This gave Captain Haldane an idea. He resolved to go into hiding beneath the floor, so that the Boers should think he had escaped, and then, when the officers were moved and the building was left empty, to emerge and get out of the town. His companions in the attempt were Lieutenant Neil Le Mesurier of the Dublin Fusiliers and Sergeant-Major A. Brockie of the Imperial Light Horse. They collected a few necessary articles, opened the trap-door, and went to earth.

It was a horrible place in which they found themselves. The floor of the building was about 2½ feet above the ground, and the space below was divided into five narrow compartments by four stone walls, on which the cross beams rested. Each of these compartments was about 18 feet long and 3½ feet wide, and there were manholes between them. The air, what there was of it, came through a small ventilator somewhere on the veranda. The place was pitch dark, and the atmosphere was stuffy to the last degree.

The three thought that their imprisonment there would only last for twenty-four hours. They went to earth on 26th February, and next day there was a great to-do about their disappearance. Descriptions of them were circulated over the whole country. One of their friends above, Lieutenant Frankland of the Dublin Fusiliers, arranged a small daily supply of provisions. Alas! the twenty-four hours passed and there was no move above. For nineteen days the three men remained in that horrible dungeon. Their only exercise was crawling about, in which they broke their heads constantly against beams and walls. They were covered with dirt, for very little water could be passed through the trap-door. Still they managed to endure. By the light of a dip they played games of patience and talked, and their chief anxiety was lest by snoring or talking in their sleep they should give their hiding-place away. Their friends above who were in the secret tried to persuade them to come up occasionally to get some fresh air, but they were determined to play the game according to its rigour, and refused.

But the situation was getting serious, for all three were falling ill. Captain Haldane wrote to a fellow-prisoner in the school above, a Dutch pastor called Adrian Hofmeyer, begging him to try and get the move expedited. Hofmeyer did his best with the authorities, telling them the story of a bogus rising of the prisoners; but still nothing happened. At last came the good news that the move was fixed for Friday, 16th March. The prisoners underground heard the commandant going his rounds for the last time. Then their friends gave the agreed signal, and Frankland's voice said, "Good-bye." At a quarter-past ten the prisoners were heard leaving the school, and by midday the servants and baggage had left. The three stayed below till nightfall and then walked out of the empty building. Walking is, indeed, a misnomer, for they seemed to have lost the use of their legs. They fell repeatedly and reeled like drunken men. It was not till they had got out of the town that they recovered the use of their limbs.

They had 300 miles of a difficult journey to make to safety, and surely never in the history of escapes have three men started out on a wilder enterprise in worse physical condition. Mr. Churchill had been out of training, but his physique at the time was that of an athlete's compared to Captain Haldane and his companions. Brockie, who had lived in the country and knew the language, got himself up like a wounded Boer, with his left arm in a sling and the Boer colours round his head. The trio presented the appearance of the worst kind of Irish moonlighters.

In the suburbs a special constable looked at them suspiciously, but was reassured by the sight of Brockie's wounded arm. They struck the Delagoa Bay Railway and stumbled along it, Le Mesurier having the bad luck to sprain his ankle. Their one advantage was that, having been supposed to escape three weeks before, the immediate hue and cry after them had died down.

Their first halting-place was near a station on the line, 13 miles east of Pretoria. There they lay up, suffering much from mosquitoes, and when darkness came made for the highroad running east. The Transvaal highways at that time were not like those of to-day, but simply raw red scars running across the veld, by no means easy to follow in the darkness. On this second night of their travels they were hunted by dogs, and Haldane and Le Mesurier took refuge in a stream, cowering up to their necks. Here they lost Brockie, but fortunately he was the one of the three best able to fend for himself, as he knew the country and could speak both Dutch and Kaffir. The two, soaked to the skin, spent the rest of the night in a clump of bracken, after taking a dose of quinine and opium. At daybreak they found themselves stiff with rheumatism. They had finished their whisky, and the provisions, matches, and tobacco were soaked.

At dawn, in a tremendous thunderstorm, they made for the railway again, and there Haldane, to his consternation, discovered that he had left his money and belt in the last hiding-place. He dared not return for them, even if he had had any hope of finding the place again. So there were the two men, without food or money, weary, cramped, and sick, with the better part of 300 miles before them in an enemy country.

Food must be found, and that night they came on a Kafir kraal with a field of water melons. They made a meal off the melons and stumbled on again. The next night their physical condition began to be really serious. In four nights they had only covered 36 miles, and their food was reduced to one tin of pemmican, one tin of cocoa, and a scrap of biltong. They had hoped for mealies from the fields, but the mealie harvest had just been gathered and not a cob remained. Another misfortune was the condition of the veld grass. They had expected it to be long enough to hide in, but it was far too short for shelter, and they were therefore compelled to lie up by day in wet swamps.

That night, having finished every scrap of food, they blundered into a Kafir hut beside a coal-siding, where some natives were eating mealie-meal porridge. Their only course was to reveal themselves, for the Kafirs were in the main on the British side. They learned that the natives' master, the manager of the coal-mine, was a Dane, and to him they disclosed their identity. The manager was friendly. He said his own mine was sending no coals to the coast for the moment, but that at a colliery next door three trucks were being loaded up for Delagoa Bay next morning. He handed his visitors over to the storekeeper of the mine, Mr. Moore, who gave them a dry bed and a good meal.

Next morning they heard that the mine doctor, a Scotsman called Gillespie, was coming to see them, and in him they found a stout ally, for he knew all about their escape, and had been looking for their arrival in order to help them. He was one of the people who had already assisted Mr. Churchill. That evening he undertook to drive them to another mine, where a plan of escape could be matured.

In the early darkness they drove 14 miles over the veld to the colliery of the Transvaal Delagoa Bay Company. There they were handed over to Mr. J. E. Howard, who had been the chief agent in Mr. Churchill's escape. There, too, they were introduced to Mr. Addams, the secretary of the mine, who turned out to be no other than the Englishman with the St. Bernard dog who had been accustomed to walk past the Staats Model School. He and the manager of the mine store, Mr. Burnham, at once set about planning their escape. It was arranged that Mr. Howard should feign illness for a few days and remain indoors, and that Haldane and Le Mesurier should take up their quarters with him. To their relief they also got news of Brockie, for he had turned up a little earlier at the same place, and had been given a passport to the border.

The plan arranged was as follows: Wool was still being sent down from the high veld to Delagoa Bay, and the trucks for it were usually detached at Middelburg. It was arranged that Burnham should buy a truck-load of wool and wire to a firm at Delagoa Bay offering the consignment. This was done, wires were exchanged, and sixteen bales of wool were duly collected and consigned to the coast. The truck for the wool was brought up the line and carefully loaded. The bales, each of which weighed 400 lb., were so arranged that there was a kind of tunnel at the bottom down the centre, in which the fugitives could hide. From behind the blinds in the sickroom of Mr. Howard, Haldane and Le Mesurier watched with acute interest the last stages of these preparations.

At 5 a.m. one morning they climbed into the tunnel below the wool, where their friends had provided them with ample provisions for a week in the shape of roast duck and chicken, beef and bread, butter and jam, nine bottles of cold tea, two of water, and one of whisky. The tarpaulin was made fast over the top, and for five hours the two waited. At ten o'clock that morning Mr. Howard came along and took a final farewell. A certain Field-Cornet Pretorius had arrived that morning and had shown himself very suspicious about the tablecloth in Mr. Howard's dining-room, but the manager had explained it with the story of a dinner and card party. By midday the truck was taken by a colliery engine to Whitbank station. Mr. Addams and Mr. Burnham were on the look-out there, and to their horror saw the Dutch driver and stoker stroll up and lean against the truck. They endeavoured to draw them away by offers of drinks; but the driver would not move, and taking a paper from his pocket began to conduct his correspondence against the side of the truck. A sneeze or a word from inside would have given away the whole plan. Even when the man left the danger was not over, for while the truck was being shunted, one of the station officials actually undid the tarpaulin and looked in, but saw nothing.

At 2.30 p.m. they were attached to a passenger train, and for the rest of the day jogged across the high veld, till at Waterval Boven, where the descent to the low veld begins, the train drew up for the night. They started again next morning, and presently they reached the last Transvaal station, Komati Poort, where a bridge spans the Komati river. This was the place where a search was likely, and to the intense disappointment of the fugitives they found the truck detached and pushed into a siding. Discovery seemed now certain, and Haldane decided to try and bribe the first comer. He got a bag of a hundred sovereigns ready, and destroyed any compromising matter in his diary.

As it happened, the Pretoria Government had wired to Komati Poort to order the strictest search of all goods trucks. The stowaways heard the unloosening of the ropes of their tarpaulin, and down in their tunnel realized it had been lifted up and thrown back. They saw daylight flood in at the tunnel end, and believed that at any moment the face of a station official would look down on them. Then to their amazement the tarpaulin was returned to its place. They may not have been seen ; or a Kafir may have caught a glimpse of them, and, having no desire to aid the law, said nothing.

But though the tarpaulin was drawn again, their suspense was not over. All that day and all the following night they lay there, anxious, half stifled, and now very hungry, for they had thrown away most of their provisions, believing that they would not be needed. Saturday morning came, and they realized that they had hoped the day before to be inside the Portuguese border. At last, at 9 a.m., the train steamed off, and while crossing the Komati bridge the two men shook hands. They saw the white pillar which marked the boundary, and realized that they had won freedom.

The train stopped at the first Portuguese station; but the two stowaways did not dare to alight. They waited till the evening and then crept out in the dusk. At a Kafir kraal close by they learned that the hotel there was kept by two Englishmen, and thither they stumbled. In five minutes they were in a back room being regaled with champagne by their excited compatriots.

Brockie had also escaped, but all three paid for some time the penalty of their wild adventure with malaria, and in the case of Le Mesurier with enteric. In a few weeks, however, they were back on duty at the front. Captain Haldane, as we have seen, was to rise to be one of the most successful British generals in the Great War. Brockie was killed by a mining accident a few years later after the escape. Le Mesurier fell at the Second Battle of Ypres, and Frankland, who had assisted them to escape, died in a reconnaissance at the Dardanelles.

Kafir kraals.

V

THE ESCAPE OF PRINCE CHARLES EDWARD

WHEN, on April 16, 1746, the clans were broken on Culloden Moor, the first thought of loyal hearts was for the safety of the Prince's person. The Rising had terrified the Government of George II., for it had won a glamour and a success which no one had believed to be within the bounds of possibility, and the glamour was created by the personality of Charles Edward. From a boy he had dreamed one dream and hoped one hope, and he had never ceased to see in solemn vision the crown placed upon his father's head by his own hands, and his father's subjects delivered by his own sword from a usurper's tyranny. When he was about twenty, a young Scottish poet, a member of a great Whig family which had been the enemy of his house, was visiting Rome. The Prince, who made it his business to know all about British travellers in Italy, found the young Scotsman in the Capitol, and laying his hand on his shoulder, addressed him by name. "Mr. Hamilton, do you like this prospect, or the one from North Berwick Law best?" North Berwick Law was near the home of Hamilton's Whig relatives, but early prejudices vanished before the charm of the Prince's manner and conversation, and Charles Edward had gained a recruit for his future army.

This personal fascination had been the real strength

of the Jacobite cause from the moment of the Prince's landing in Scotland. There had been great expectations of French help, and when these seemed likely to fail, Prince Charlie had said in 1744, " I will be in Scotland next summer, though it is with a single footman." Next summer, he had landed on the little island of Eriskay with seven men. His small following alarmed the few friends who met him. The task seemed hopeless, and they advised him to return home. " I am come home," he replied, and gave orders to sail to the mainland.

His personal appeal led men to join him in defiance of every dictate of interest and common-sense. " I will erect the royal standard," he said to Cameron of Lochiel, " and proclaim to the people of Britain that Charles Stuart is come over to claim the crown of his ancestors, to win it, or perish in the attempt. Lochiel, who, my father has often told me, was our firmest friend, may stay at home and learn from the newspapers the fate of his Prince." The words changed Lochiel's mind. " I will share the fate of my Prince," he replied. " Will not *you* assist me ? " Charles asked another young Highlander, and drew the expected answer, " I will, though no other man in the Highlands should draw his sword." Throughout the whole campaign, it was the Prince who maintained the Jacobite army ; hope and inspiration came from him, and his were the fleeting triumphs that brightened the early months of an effort foredoomed to failure. " I leave for England in eight days," he said in Edinburgh, " England will be ours in two months ; " and in the Council of War at Derby his voice alone was given for the march to London : " to put it to the test and win or lose it all." After the retreat and the victory at Falkirk, Charles wished to remain in the Lowlands and meet Cumberland there. He hoped to the end, and refused to seek safety in flight while he had still an army to fight for him.

On his arrival the Government had offered a reward of £30,000 for his head, and tradition tells that the Prince wished to retort by offering £30 as an adequate sum for the head of the Elector of Hanover. Even in the hour of defeat at Culloden, his followers felt that the ministers of King George would still be eager to secure the person of an enemy, whose charm and fascination had wrought one miracle and might be employed to work another. While the Prince was still a free man, could the House of Hanover be safe? The savage Duke of Cumberland would certainly wish to add to his tarnished laurels the glory of the capture of the fugitive. There was little time for consideration; the battle was fought and lost in less than half an hour, and Cumberland's fresh troops might be trusted to be active in the pursuit. The Prince would not believe that all was lost, and he tried to induce the stragglers to return to the charge. Those nearest to him begged him not to expose his person needlessly, for the broken clans would not rally. He hesitated, and one of them seized his bridle and turned his horse's head to the rear, just as, a hundred years before, his great-grandfather, Charles I., had been led off the field of Naseby with the words, "Will you go upon your death?"

I

IN BADENOCH AND LOCHABER

For a few minutes it seemed as if the Prince were still "going upon" his death. The fire of Cumberland's artillery did not slacken as the Jacobite army wavered, and the retreating Prince had his horse shot under him. A groom brought him a fresh horse, and, as he mounted, the man fell dead by his side. Whither was he to flee? No plan had been made for the event of a defeat, and no rendezvous had been appointed for the beaten army. Accompanied by a few friends, and a body-guard of some fifty horse, he rode off towards the river Nairn. His direction was southwards, and Cumberland was pushing the pursuit westwards to Inverness, but had detached a body of horse to ride down the stragglers. Charles left the field blinded with tears that fell for his lost hopes, and he very narrowly escaped falling in with this force as he pursued his uncertain way.

His bonnet fell from his head, and a private in his Life Guards brought him another. It was Edward Burke, whom the Prince recognized as a servant of one of his aides-de-camp. Burke belonged to an Irish family which, for some generations, had been settled in the Hebrides, and he was a native of North Uist. When he joined the army he was a "chairman" (the carrier of a sedan chair) in Edinburgh, but he had been a gentleman's servant, and had travelled much with his master, and he knew the country. "Ned," said the Prince, "if you be a true friend, lead us safe off." Ned, greatly honoured, did his best, and was the wanderer's first guide. Ned Burke was described by those who knew him as true as steel but a rough man, and he addressed the Prince with the wonted familiarity of the Scottish peasantry. Charles humoured him and chaffed him, and they had a standing joke about "Deil speed the leears (liars)," a wish obviously appropriate to a disguised prince and his companions.

When Ned took command of the party, the Prince dismissed his body-guard, and with Ned's master and five others he crossed the Nairn and rode for some distance up the right bank. It was growing late and they sought refuge at Tordarroch, but in vain, and pushing on, they recrossed the river near Aberarder, where they were again refused entrance. Both of these places were too near Inverness for safety. It was fortunate that they did not halt until they reached the hamlet of Gortuleg, where, in a house still in existence, they found the aged Lord Lovat, the Fox of the Highlands, who had played false to both sides, and was attempting to escape from the fate that was to overtake him on Tower Hill. The Prince drank three glasses of wine with Lovat, who reminded him that Robert the Bruce had lost eleven battles and won Scotland by the twelfth. Doubtful history, and a moral which could not be acted upon, were poor consolation, and Charles speedily left his host and rode on through the night.

There was some moonlight—the moon was in her first quarter—and the tired little company reached Invergarry Castle just as the moon was setting. The house was empty and there was no food ; but the Prince had some rest, and Ned Burke noticed a fishing net which had been set, and found two salmon, which he cooked for their breakfast. In the afternoon they took to their horses again and rode along Loch Arkaig to Glenpean, where they spent the night. Next day the Prince expected a communication from his friends or a hint of the doings of his pursuers, but none came. Cumberland, in fact, was on the wrong track. He thought that the fugitive had made his way to Lovat's country near Beauly, and the real route was unknown to the enemy. Making for the sea, the Prince walked from Glenpean over the hills to the beautiful region of Morar, had some sleep in a lonely shieling, and through the night of the 20th April tramped to Borrodale, in Arisaig, where he had landed nine months before.

Less than a fortnight later, two French vessels, carrying gold, reached Borrodale, but the Prince was no longer there. He had stayed for five days, but he could not know where his safety lay, and his friends had sent him a fresh guide in the person of a Skye farmer named Donald MacLeod. The Prince went out to meet Donald and they had their first conversation alone in a wood. His new friend was horror-struck at the Prince's first suggestion. Like his ancestress Queen Mary, Charles was seized with a mad desire to throw himself on the mercy of his enemies. He did not, indeed, propose to surrender to Cumberland's troops, but he asked Donald to carry letters for him to his own chief, MacLeod, and to Sir Alexander MacDonald of Sleat. These men were on the Government side, but he believed that they would do everything in their power for his safety. Donald replied that his life was at the Prince's command, but that nothing would induce him thus to reveal his whereabouts. "Does not your Excellency know that these men have played the rogue to you altogether, and will you trust them for a' that? Na, you maunna do't." Then Donald told him that the Laird of MacLeod and Sir Alexander MacDonald were searching for him about twelve miles away by sea, and urged that the sooner he left Borrodale the better. Donald was a skilful seaman, and he undertook to conduct the Prince to the Hebrides, in the hope of finding a ship to take him to France.

It was not good advice, for a British fleet commanded the seas, and the islands were easily watched. The best hiding-place was in the wild district of Morar, whence, as we have seen, he could have escaped within a fortnight. But he could not tell that his refuge might not be discovered. It was quite well known among the people, for Donald's son Murdoch, an Inverness schoolboy, who had run away from school to fight at Culloden, astonished his father by appearing at Borrodale; he had traced and followed the Prince, and less friendly inquirers might do the same. Charles thought of the £30,000 reward, and as yet he did not realize that the Highlanders were not thinking about it. He spent five more unhappy and restless days at Borrodale, while Donald MacLeod obtained a boat and a crew. At last an eight-oared boat was ready, with eight boatmen, among whom were Ned Burke and the boy, Murdoch MacLeod. The Prince's companions were Captain O'Sullivan, Captain O'Neil, Captain Allan MacDonald, and a Roman priest. Donald MacLeod was skipper, and he is known to history as the Prince's Pilot.

On the evening of 26th April the Pilot warned the Prince that a great storm was coming, and begged him not to sail; but Charles was anxious about the parties which were searching for him on the mainland, and he insisted. They were unobserved by any of the Government vessels; indeed, the fleet had gone off to the remote island of St. Kilda, misled by some rumour that the Prince was there. But the Pilot's prophecy was fulfilled; he said afterwards that the tempest was more violent than any "he had ever been trysted with before, though all his life a seafaring man." Thunder and lightning and torrential rain, a hurricane, and a heavy sea, were a new experience for a Prince in an open boat. "I had rather face cannons and muskets than be in such a storm as this," he said, and told Donald to make again for the shore. To obey the command would have been certain death. "Since we are here," said the Pilot, "we have nothing for it but, under God, to set out to sea. Is it not as good for us to be drowned in clean water as to be dashed in pieces upon a rock and to be drowned too?" So they made for the open sea; it was pitch dark, they had neither lantern nor compass nor even a pump. Through the whole night scarcely a man spoke one word; the thought of all was that it would be better to be drowned in clean water than to be driven on the coast of Skye, where bodies of militiamen were on the outlook for the wanderer.

II

IN THE OUTER ISLES

Morning broke, and the storm was still raging, but they were far beyond the shores of Skye. They succeeded in landing at Rossinish in Benbecula, and found an uninhabited hut in which they lit a fire and dried their clothes. In this desolate region they remained two days, and on the night of 29th April set sail for the island of Scalpa, the tenant of which, Donald Campbell, was a friend of the Pilot. They agreed to represent themselves as the captain and crew of a ship which had been wrecked on the island of Tiree. O'Sullivan took the name of Captain Sinclair, and the Prince passed as young Sinclair, his son. They were hospitably received at Scalpa, and their host, Donald Campbell, was in the secret of the shipwrecked crew. They were eager, they said, to return to their home in the Orkneys, and sent the Pilot to Stornoway to hire a vessel.

Meanwhile, mischief was brewing. John Macaulay, minister of South Uist (grandfather of Lord Macaulay), had heard of the Prince's coming, and he informed his father, Aulay Macaulay, minister of Harris. The Macaulays were strong Whigs, and there is a tradition that, while Prince Charlie was in Scalpa, Aulay Macaulay and a neighbouring laird landed in the island with a boatful of armed men and announced their intention of earning the blood-money which the Government had offered. But Donald Campbell warned the Prince and his followers, and told the invaders that he would himself fall in the Prince's cause rather than give up a man who had entrusted him with his life, and Macaulay and his friends "sneaked off the island." At all events, the information sent by John Macaulay (who long afterwards was snubbed at Inveraray by Dr. Johnson) spoiled the plan of the ship-wrecked mariners. When Donald MacLeod reached Stornoway, he found difficulty in securing a ship and suspected that the truth was known ; but at last he succeeded in buying one and sent the good news to Scalpa.

On 4th May the Prince, with O'Sullivan, O'Neil, and Ned Burke, crossed to Harris. The journey was unfortunate, for they were misled by a guide whom they had engaged, and they tramped all night through wind and rain. The Pilot met them and told them that he had arranged for their reception at Kildun House, two miles from Stornoway, and he himself returned to the town to make final preparations. To his surprise, he found the road barred by two or three hundred men in arms, who explained that they knew the Prince was coming with a force of five hundred men to seize a vessel in Stornoway, and that they feared the vengeance of the Government. He told them the truth, and they disowned any intention of doing the Prince an injury, but insisted on his taking his departure. It was in vain that Donald asked for a guide who knew these stormy seas, and he had to return and tell the news. The boat had followed them, though two of the boatmen had deserted, and on the morning of 6th May they set sail for Scalpa.

As they approached the island they had the "comfort and mortification" of seeing, without being observed, three Government vessels on the outlook, and they changed their course for the desert island of Euirn or Iubhard, where they found some fishermen who had erected little huts, like pigsties, for a temporary shelter. The fishermen mistook the newcomers for a press-gang from the war-ships and fled, but they left their fish behind them, and the fugitives had brought some provisions. They remained for four days on this desolate island, occupying one of the "pigsties." It rained hard and they had to cover the hut with the boat-sail for shelter, but the Prince was in excellent spirits. He insisted on doing the cooking himself, and laughed at Ned Burke for being too fine to eat butter which had got mixed up with bread-crumbs. A large stone served as a table for the Prince and the gentlemen, and the boatmen ate by themselves. Leaving this retreat on 10th May, they returned to Scalpa, but found that their kind host had been compelled to flee, and that it was not safe for them to remain.

It was after leaving Scalpa that the Prince had his first narrow escape. They were sailing south along the coast of Harris, when, near Finsbay, they found themselves within two musket shots of a man-of-war under full sail. Their little boat was itself under full sail and the boatmen rowed for dear life. "I will never be taken alive," said the Prince as the race went on. They were hotly pursued for three leagues, until they reached shallow water near Rodil Point, where their enemy could not follow them as they sailed among the creeks. After an ineffectual attempt, he turned his course out to sea, and they hugged the coast until they reached Loch Maddy. There they spied another war-ship, but retreated from the loch without attracting observation, and that night (11th May) they landed on an island in Loch Uskavagh in Benbecula. During their two days' sail they were short of food, and the Prince, who had given his followers some lessons in cooking at Euirn, was taught how to make drammock, that is, meal mixed with water—salt water unfortunately. He ate heartily of it, and his Pilot loved to tell how "never any meat or drink came wrong to him, for he could take a share of everything, be it good, bad, or indifferent, and was always cheerful and contented in every condition."

There was need of cheerfulness, for though, as they were landing in the rain, one of the boatmen captured a crab and waved it triumphantly at the Prince, the hut, which was their only refuge, was so low that they had to dig below the door and line the hole with heather for the Prince to crawl through. The hut, said the Prince, had been inhabited by the devil, who had left it because he had not room enough in it. After three days in this island, they crossed to South Uist and walked to Coradale, where Charles had more comfortable quarters in a cottage. He was delighted with his new abode and sat on a turf seat smoking a pipe very happily until bedtime. The three weeks spent at Coradale were the least troubled period of his wanderings. He was a good shot, and brought down a deer one day "firing off-hand"; he also fished from a small boat with a hand-line. The weather was fine, and he often sat on a stone by the door, basking in the sunshine and watching the ships pass; he deluded himself with the hope that they were French, but his friends knew that they were on the watch for him. Occasionally he was melancholy, but he would recover, and dance for a whole hour together to the music of a Highland reel, which he whistled as he tripped along.

The happy days did not last long; the Government troops returned from their vain journey to St. Kilda, and Barra and Uist began to be dangerous. Donald MacLeod, the Pilot, had been sent to the mainland and returned with news and two ankers of brandy, in time to accompany the Prince in the flight which was rendered necessary by the presence of troops in the neighbourhood. On 6th June they sailed to the island of Ouia or Wiay, about twelve miles distant, but they were not yet safe, and returned to Rossinish in Benbecula, fortunately not taking the Pilot with them. At Rossinish Charles was in grave danger, for he was warned to make his escape, and the passage to Ouia was guarded by Government vessels. Taking advantage of the short midsummer hours of darkness or twilight, Donald MacLeod brought a boat to the rescue, and they made for their old retreat at Coradale; but a storm and a glimpse of two war-ships forced them to land where they could, and the Prince slept in a cleft of a rock, drawing his bonnet over his eyes for shelter. The storm continued to rage all next day, but the enemy were within two miles of them, and at night they found another refuge. Their hope was to reach the territory of MacDonald of Boisdale, who, they believed, could help them, and on 15th June they sailed for Boisdale in South Uist.

It was a dangerous journey, for fifteen sail were visible at sea, and they knew that the land was guarded. They lay all day out of sight in a narrow creek, and landed at night on the shores of Loch Boisdale, where the Prince slept on a bed of heather in the shelter of a ruined castle. Next morning their spirits rose, for the Pilot saw two French ships appearing, and they were ready to hail them when they made the sad discovery that they were Government vessels. A party of soldiers under Captain Caroline Scott, one of Cumberland's best executioners, landed within a mile of them, and the Prince took to the hills, while the boatmen concealed the boat. For three days the Prince was engaged in dodging the Redcoats on one side or the other of Loch Boisdale. Their journey was useless, for Boisdale had been made a prisoner, and his wife could do no more than warn them of Scott's neighbourhood.

The Prince decided on a bold and desperate plan. When he was at Coradale, a half-hearted friend, Ronald MacDonald, the chief of Clanranald, had sent him as an attendant a gentleman of his clan named Neil Macdonald-Maceachain, the future father of a distinguished son, Napoleon's Marshal Macdonald, Duke of Tarentum. Neil Maceachain had been educated in France for the priesthood, and Clanranald knew that he was fitted to be a companion for the Prince. Soon after Neil joined him, the Prince received a message from Hugh Macdonald of Armadale. This man was in

A storm and a glimpse of two war-ships forced them to land.

See page 90.

charge of a company under his cousin, Sir Alexander Macdonald of Sleat, whose duty was to capture the Prince. But Hugh Macdonald had served in the French army and was himself a Jacobite, and his loyalty to his own chief was modified by the circumstance that his chief's wife, Lady Margaret MacDonald, was known to sympathize with the Prince's cause. Some years before he had abducted, or eloped with, the young widow of Ranald MacDonald of Milton in South Uist, and his stepdaughter, Flora MacDonald, was living with her brother at Milton. The message which he sent to the Prince contained a warning that, since the Government forces knew him to be concealed in the Outer Hebrides, it was hopeless to try and elude them, and offered a suggestion of an escape to Skye, where Lady Margaret would receive him in her husband's absence. The plan was that Hugh MacDonald should give his stepdaughter a pass or safe-conduct to her mother's house in Skye, that the Prince should be disguised as her maid, and that Neil Maceachain should accompany them as a servant.

When Charles, with Captain O'Neil and Neil Maceachain, was in hiding on the top of one of the mountains overlooking Loch Boisdale, this scheme recurred to his mind, and, on 21st June, the three walked to within a short distance of a shieling where Flora MacDonald and her brother were tending their cattle. That evening the Prince, who had just parted with his faithful Pilot and with Ned Burke, had his first interview with the brave girl whose name was to be so honourably linked with his own. He himself told her of her stepfather's proposal, and she answered that she would gladly take the risk. It had to be then or never, and Flora set out at once for Benbecula to arrange matters with her stepfather and to procure a disguise from Lady Clanranald, while the Prince and his two followers found shelter in the hills near his old quarters at Coradale. Next day, the impatient Prince sent Neil Maceachain to Benbecula to bring back a report; but when he came to the fords between South Uist and Benbecula, he found that they were closely guarded at low tide, when alone they are passable. Flora MacDonald had met with the same difficulty the preceding day, and each of them asked to be taken to the captain of the company, who was Hugh MacDonald. Neil found Flora breakfasting with her step-father, and they arranged that Neil and the Prince should meet her at Rossinish. The difficulty was to bring him there; they dared not risk an attempt to pass by the fords. But Neil was lucky enough to find some fishermen whom he knew, and they ferried the Prince and Captain O'Neil and himself to the coast of Benbecula, in the darkness, and left them on a tidal island, much to the alarm of the Prince, who awoke from a sound sleep to find himself upon a small rock surrounded by water.

At low tide they made their way to the shore, and after a cold wet night in the heather, set out for Rossinish in a wild storm of wind and rain. Walking was very difficult, and the exhausted Prince was constantly falling into holes concealed by the heather or losing his shoes in the bogs. At last they reached the rendezvous, and Neil went on to reconnoitre. He did not find Flora or Lady Clanranald, and he was informed that twenty of the Skye militiamen were in a tent about a quarter of a mile away. There seemed nothing for it but another night in the heather, but they found shelter at some little distance, in a house belonging to a tenant of Clanranald. At dawn their hostess turned them out because she knew the militiamen were coming to buy milk, and they hid themselves under a rock by the shore. The rain never ceased, and they thought that all the windows of heaven had been broken open. The rock was an insufficient protection, and a swarm of midges settled upon the Prince's face and hands, inflicting such misery that he cried out in his pain and despair. At last, they were told that the militia had gone; they returned to a warm room and a bright fire; the Prince hung up his clothes to dry, sat at the fireside in his shirt "as merry and hearty as if he was in the best room at Whitehall," and slept contentedly upon the door, which was taken down and covered with a ragged sail to make a bed for him.

Two days later, on the evening of 27th June, Flora MacDonald arrived with her brother and Lady Clanranald and Captain O'Neil, who had gone in search of the ladies. They sat down to a good supper, but had scarcely begun when a herd rushed breathlessly into the room and told them that General Campbell was landing his men three miles away. In a few minutes they were in the boat, and they spent the night crossing Loch Uskavagh and finished their supper on the other side at five o'clock in the morning. Lady Clanranald then returned to Benbecula to plead with General Campbell to spare her home. Flora's brother went with her, and Flora insisted that Captain O'Neil should accompany them. She disliked the attentions he paid her, and she knew that his presence would draw fresh suspicion upon her little company, which was to consist of the Prince, Neil Maceachain, and herself. Her stepfather's passport was for herself and her servant, and for a woman named Betty Burke, an expert with the spinning-wheel. As an additional precaution, Hugh MacDonald had furnished her with a letter to his wife, saying that Betty's services should be secured for the spinning of a large quantity of lint which was in the house at Armadale.

Before Lady Clanranald left, she, with Flora MacDonald's help, dressed the Prince in the clothes they had prepared for him. He laughed and the lady wept as they clad him in the coarse garb of a gentlewoman's servant—a light-coloured quilted petticoat, a flowered calico gown, a white apron, and a long dark cloak made of the rough homespun known as camlet. The head-dress was large enough to cover his whole head and face. Charles was much amused by the apron, and kept telling them not to forget it.

At eight o'clock on the evening of 28th June, Flora, with Betty Burke and Neil Maceachain, set sail from Benbecula for Skye. The sea was rough, but the Prince was in great spirits, and he sang the Cavalier songs which told of the Restoration of his great-uncle, Charles II.—"The Twenty-ninth of May" and "The King shall Enjoy his Own Again." Flora MacDonald fell asleep, and he kept guard lest any of the boatmen should stumble over her in the darkness.

III

IN SKYE

Next morning they were off the coast of Skye with a heavy gale in their faces. They were about to land at the point of Waternish, when they saw two sentries, one of whom ordered them to stop. They rowed out to sea as fast as they could; he fired and missed them, and his companion went off to give the alarm. Fifteen men came up, and two boats were lying ready. Pursuit and capture seemed inevitable, for the Prince had no arms, but the soldiers were content with walking along the shore and watching the direction taken by the little boat, and, after hiding in a creek, Flora and her companions landed undisturbed at Kilbride, in Troternish, near Monkstat, the house of Sir Alexander MacDonald of Sleat. The laird, as they knew, was with Cumberland at Fort Augustus, but they were sure of help from Lady Margaret.

Flora Macdonald took Neil with her to Monkstat, and left the Prince in the boat. The boatmen were instructed, if any inquiry should be made about the person in the boat, to answer that it was a maid of

Miss MacDonald's, a lazy jade who would not follow her mistress. At Monkstat Flora obtained a private interview with Lady Margaret, and found that there were two guests in the house—MacDonald of Kingsburgh, Sir Alexander's factor or land agent, and Lieutenant Alexander MacLeod, who was in command of the party which had so nearly caught the Prince. Lady Margaret sent for Kingsburgh and told him the story. It was impossible to risk a meeting between Betty Burke and Lieutenant MacLeod, and he promised to take the Prince to his own house at Kingsburgh. Neil was sent to convoy the Prince from the boat to a hill a mile from Monkstat, and a bundle of clothes was prepared in order that Betty Burke might be seen to carry her mistress's baggage. They reached the tryst-ing-place in safety, and the Prince sent Neil back to the boat for a case of knives which would have aroused suspicion if it had been found by the enemy. Neil reluctantly left him within a gun-shot of the highroad, and returned to find that Kingsburgh had brought him wine and biscuits. He had tracked him through noticing a number of sheep running away as if alarmed by a stranger, a hint which, fortunately, was not taken by any of the soldiers who were moving about.

Lady Margaret's problem was to lull any suspicions of her other guest, and for this purpose Flora MacDonald dined at Monkstat, and had a conversation with Lieutenant MacLeod, who was anxious to know if, in her journey from Benbecula, she had heard anything about the movements of Charles Edward. She gave discreet answers to his inquiries, and, in his presence, Lady Margaret strongly opposed the suggestion that Flora should go home that night. She had often promised them a visit, and she must not leave them after a few hours. Flora begged to be excused; she was anxious to see her mother, and to be at home in these troublous times. Lady Margaret reluctantly yielded, but insisted on sending her own maid with her.

Flora set out on horseback, and soon overtook Kingsburgh, Betty Burke, and Neil. Some of the neighbours followed her and were much interested in Betty. They remarked on the impudence with which she walked and talked with Kingsburgh, and were indignant that he should make a serving-woman his companion and pay no attention to her mistress. They observed her masculine walk, and were much shocked by the carelessness with which she raised her skirts when fording a stream. Neil pacified them by saying that she was an Irish girl, whom Miss Flora had picked up in Uist and had brought home because of her marvellous skill in spinning. At last they shook off their inquisitive companions, and the little party reached Kingsburgh House about midnight.

The mistress of the house had gone to bed, and was roused by the visit of an excited daughter, " O mother, my father has brought in such a very odd, muckle, ill-shaken-up wife as ever I saw! " Mrs. MacDonald went down and found Betty Burke traversing the hall with " wide, lang steps." Her husband asked her to get some supper, and Betty Burke saluted her with a kiss from unshaven lips. Kingsburgh followed her and told her that they had the Prince as a guest. They agreed that it was a hanging matter, but resolved to die in a good cause, and the lady's anxiety was diverted from the gallows by the difficulty of providing a supper fit for a prince. She brought him roasted eggs and bread and butter, and he drank two bottles of small beer and a bumper of brandy. Then he produced a cracked pipe which he had tied up with thread, and asked for tobacco, which Kingsburgh gave him—along with a new pipe.

In the morning the Prince slept late, and Flora and Kingsburgh took counsel together. They knew the amiable methods of the soldiery, and were sure that the boatmen, threatened with torture, would tell the story of Betty Burke. Though they were reluctant to disturb the Prince's rest, it was necessary to get him away at once. They roused him and dressed him in his female attire, for it was obviously desirable that he should leave the house in his disguise, so that any information which leaked out through the servants might lead his pursuers to watch for a man in woman's clothes. Before he left, Flora cut a lock from his hair, and his hostess gave him a silver snuff-box engraved with two clasped hands and the motto "Rob Gib." Some days later the Prince noticed the motto, asked a companion what it meant, and was told that Rob Gib's contract was stark love and kindness. "I will keep it all my life," he said.

Kingsburgh accompanied him on his way, and, in a wood, Betty Burke changed into Highland dress, and "with a claymore in his hand he was a soger-like man indeed." Bidding farewell to Kingsburgh with the words, "I am afraid I shall not meet another MacDonald in my difficulties," he and Neil Maceachain walked to Portree under the guidance of a little boy. He left Kingsburgh just in time, for Monkstat and Kingsburgh House were soon searched by the fierce General Ferguson, who insulted Mrs. MacDonald and met her denials of the Prince's presence with the remark that she had put the maid in a better room than her mistress. Cumberland was furious at the Prince's escape, and ordered the arrest of Kingsburgh, who, he said, had neglected the greatest service which could have been done to King George. The Prince's host spent twelve months in prison as the reward of one night's hospitality.

At Kingsburgh Charles had again proposed to throw himself on the mercy of MacLeod, but had been persuaded to fall in with an arrangement made by Lady Margaret and Kingsburgh. One of Sir Alexander MacDonald's clan, Donald Roy MacDonald, had been prevented by his chief from going to the Prince when he raised his standard, but had joined after the battle of

Prestonpans, had been wounded in the foot at Culloden, and was hiding in a surgeon's house in Troternish. It was agreed at Monkstat that Donald Roy MacDonald should meet the Prince at Portree, and arrange for his crossing to the island of Raasay under the protection of the Laird of Raasay.

While Charles was at Kingsburgh, Donald Roy succeeded in finding a son of the Laird of Raasay, known by the name of his father's property of Rona, a neighbouring island. All the boats in Skye had been commandeered, and Rona had to take a crazy old boat which he found abandoned in a fresh-water loch, and to convey it to the sea, in order to obtain one of his father's boats from Raasay. Before the Prince reached Portree on 30th June, Rona had returned accompanied by his brother, Murdoch MacLeod, and by a cousin, Captain Malcolm MacLeod. Flora MacDonald performed her last service to the Prince by riding to Portree to make sure of his reception, and the whole party—the Prince, Flora MacDonald, Neil Maceachain, Donald Roy MacDonald, and the three MacLeods—met at an inn. Charles purchased a quarter of a pound of tobacco, and Donald Roy had to insist upon his taking three halfpence brought him by the landlord as change for sixpence; but in spite of this warning of the danger of arousing suspicion by unheard-of liberality, he proposed later to be satisfied with eleven shillings as change for a guinea, the landlord not being able to produce more silver. Donald Roy checked him and got the guinea changed elsewhere.

They were to sail about midnight, and the Prince made his farewells. He had always treated Flora MacDonald with the greatest deference, and invariably rose when she entered the room, and he used to speak of her as "our Lady." He kissed her—the usual salutation of the time. "For all that has happened," he said, "I hope, madam, we shall meet in St. James's yet." Nine days had elapsed since they first met in the shieling in South Uist; for three days they had been fellow-wanderers. He was not destined to receive her at St. James's, nor ever to see her again after their parting in the village inn, but a gracious recollection of "our Lady" can never have been obliterated by the sins and the sorrows of later years. She was again to meet a Prince of Wales, for, when she was a prisoner in London, the heir of George II. paid his respects to her and gave to history one of the few pleasant stories that are recorded of "Fred who was alive and is dead." Four years later she married Kingsburgh's son; she became the mother of many children; she entertained Dr. Johnson in the house to which she had brought Prince Charlie. Her adventures were not yet over, for, in the year after Johnson's visit, she and her husband emigrated to North Carolina, and she saw the fighting in the early campaigns of the American War. She returned to Skye and died at Kingsburgh in 1790, two years after "King Charles III." had breathed his last at Rome. Those three June days when she was the Prince's preserver have consecrated her name and her memory while courage and loyalty are deemed worthy of the reverence of mankind.

The Prince had still before him many weary wanderings. He bade good-bye that evening not only to Flora MacDonald, but also to Neil Maceachain, whom he sent to attend the Lady to her home. Donald Roy was lame and could not accompany him, and he was conducted by the two MacLeods, Murdoch and Malcolm; he went off with a bottle of whisky strapped to his belt at one side, and a bottle of brandy, some shirts, and a cold fowl on the other side. They reached Raasay safely; but the Prince thought the island too small for concealment, and during the short time they were there they were alarmed by a man whom the islanders suspected to be a spy. He came near their hut, and Malcolm MacLeod proposed to shoot him, but Charles forbade him, and the stranger passed on without looking in. The Prince insisted upon returning to Skye; he was not quite happy among the MacLeods and wished to be with Donald Roy again.

Late on the evening of 2nd July they left Raasay in a storm, the Prince singing a Highland song to cheer the boatmen; he had learned Gaelic in the course of his expedition. They landed at Scorrybreck, close to Portree, and the Prince spent an uneasy night in a cow-byre, often wakening up and looking round him with a startled air. "O poor England," he was heard to murmur in his sleep. Donald Roy had been sent for, but was unable to come, and Malcolm MacLeod warned the Prince that parties of soldiers were on the outlook, and that they must set out without a moment's delay. They walked to Mackinnon's country, the part of Skye known as Strath, and the Prince passed as MacLeod's servant and took the name of Lewie Caw, a fugitive from Culloden who was known to be hiding in Skye. Lewie Caw carried the baggage and was careful to walk behind his master and to show no curiosity when MacLeod met an acquaintance. They redoubled their precautions when they entered Mackinnon's country, because Mackinnon had been "out" and the district was specially watched. Charles exchanged his waistcoat with MacLeod because it looked too fine for a servant, and promised some day to give him a better waistcoat still when he himself should walk in London streets dressed in the kilt which Kingsburgh had given him. He removed his periwig and covered his head with a dirty napkin, but MacLeod insisted that any one who had ever seen him would know him again. "This is an odd remarkable face I have got that nothing can disguise it," he said, and MacLeod, as he looked at him, felt that no disguise could conceal his possession of "something that was not ordinary, something of the grand and stately."

In this way they reached Elgol and met the old Laird of Mackinnon, who arranged to accompany the Prince to the mainland. Malcolm MacLeod, himself a person for whom search was being made, thought that the Prince would be safer without him, and Charles reluctantly let him go, sending with him a note of thanks to Donald Roy. "Sir," it read, "I thank God I am in good health and have got off as designed. Remember me to all friends, and thank them for the trouble they have been at.—I am, Sir, your humble servant, JAMES THOMSON."

IV

IN LOCHABER

The Prince, with the old laird and his son, John Mackinnon, landed on the shore of Loch Nevis at four o'clock in the morning of 5th July, and spent three nights in the heather. On the morning of 8th July the old laird went to seek a cave as a shelter, and the Prince and John Mackinnon rowed up the loch. Suddenly, as they came round a point, their oars struck some wood, and they saw a boat tied to a rock and five men standing near it on the shore. They were at once challenged, and, when the boatmen answered that they came from Sleat, they were ordered to come ashore. They disobeyed, and the militiamen jumped into their own boat and pursued. John Mackinnon himself took an oar, for the Prince's life depended upon the race that summer morning. Charles was sitting in the bottom of the boat with his head between Mackinnon's legs. He wanted to make for the shore and trust to his powers of running; but Mackinnon spread a plaid over his head that he might not be seen, and told him firmly that he had no chance on a bare hillside, that their only hope of escape lay in their oars, and that if the pursuers came up he could rely on them all to fight to the last. Each boatman sat with a loaded musket beside him. From time to time the Prince inquired how the race was going, and Mackinnon was always able to answer that they were holding their own. It was not enough, but a desperate effort carried them round a point and out of sight of the enemy. The coast was wooded, and the Prince, Mackinnon, and one of the boatmen jumped ashore and plunged into the trees. The boat went on, but the pursuers, coming again within view, saw that their prey had escaped, and Charles, from the top of a hill, watched them return, while Mackinnon was apologizing for having disobeyed his commands. "I only wanted," he replied, "to fight for my life rather than be taken prisoner."

Later in the day they recrossed the loch and walked through the night to Morar, and MacDonald of Morar gave them his son as a guide to Borrodale. They made for the house of the Laird of Borrodale, Angus MacDonald, but it had been burned down by the troops, and they found him in a neighbouring hut. When John Mackinnon announced the Prince's presence, the old man said, "I shall lodge him so secure that all the forces in Britain shall not find him out." After his narrow escape two days before, Charles had received a cold message from Clanranald and a refusal of help from Morar, and Borrodale's welcome gave him fresh heart and hope.

The two Mackinnons left him at Borrodale, and both of them fell at once into the hands of the soldiers, who could not fail to suspect the Prince's presence in the neighbourhood. The news of their capture made old Borrodale doubly cautious, and on 13th July he hid the Prince in a cleft between two precipitous rocks where he had constructed a little hut and had covered it with green turf, so that it looked like a natural grass-covered brae. Here the Prince was joined by a nephew of his host, Alexander MacDonald of Glenaladale, who was his companion in most of what remained of his wanderings. Glenaladale had been wounded three times at Culloden, but he responded at once to the Prince's call. They did not remain long at Borrodale, for they learned that the Prince's presence in that region was known to the enemy, and they could see the ships on the coast. On 17th July they set out for a new place of concealment in Morar, where they learned that General Campbell, with six ships, had anchored in Loch Nevis, and that a party of soldiers was near them. It was clear that they were surrounded, and that they must break through the enemy's line of posts, and make for the north in the hope of finding a French ship at Poolewe, near Loch Maree.

Every day brought fresh perils and new adventures. At their first setting out they saw from the top of a hill some cattle being moved, and discovered that Glenaladale's tenants were saving their property from the troops, who were taking the very route by which the Prince had intended to go. This led them to send for a fresh guide, Donald Cameron of Glenpean, to conduct them out of the dangerous region of Morar. While they waited for him they learned that a hundred Argyllshire militiamen were at the foot of the very hill on the top of which they were resting. They could not stay for their guide, and, as the sun was setting, they moved on. A solitary figure was seen approaching them, and they could not tell whether the man was friend or foe, but, to their relief, it proved to be Donald Cameron, and he promised to lead them safely through the enemy's outposts.

From the head of Loch Eil to the head of Loch Hourn there was a long series of small camps about half a mile from each other ; the sentries were each within call of his neighbour, and patrols were constantly moving to keep the sentries alert. Cameron led them to a hill which had just been searched, and might, therefore, be regarded as safe, but they had no provisions except a little oatmeal and some butter, and, after some wanderings, they found a hiding-place for the Prince on a hill at the head of Loch Quoich, while some of the party went to get provisions. They brought back the news that a hundred redcoats were marching up the other side of the hill, and the whole party set out again towards nightfall. As they trudged along they saw in front of them a camp-fire, but they decided that they must take the risk of passing through the enemy. To remain in the region of Moidart meant certain capture. They crept along, going so near the camp that they could hear the soldiers talking, but they were unobserved. As they were climbing the next hill they came across a rivulet which, emerging from a spring, fell straight down a precipice. The Prince missed his footing and was about to fall, but was supported by Donald Cameron and Glenaladale, and they reached the top in safety, only to see another camp-fire at the foot. This they were able to avoid, but, although they had broken through the cordon, their route still lay along the line of the camps.

At the head of Loch Hourn they hid in a hollow which was covered with long heather and birch trees. They were faint with hunger, and one of them, a son of old Borrodale, produced from his pocket a small quantity of meal. He used to tell afterwards of the change produced on the faces of his companions by the sight of it. Their guide, Donald Cameron, was not sure of the way from this point, and in the evening he and Glenaladale went to find a new guide. When the two emerged from the hollow they found that they had spent the day quite close to one of the enemy's camps; they returned, and the whole party at once set out for Glenshiel. The night was very dark, and they had nothing to eat, but in the morning they got butter and cheese in a village in Glenshiel, where they were fortunate enough to find a guide, named Donald MacDonald, who had fought in the Prince's army and was fleeing from the troops. They also learned the unpleasant news that a French ship had just left Poolewe, and that it would be useless to go there. That day, 22nd July, was very hot, and they lay on a mountain side parched with thirst; a stream was near, and they could hear the sound of the water, but they dared not move. At sunset Donald Cameron bade them good-bye, and a small boy, the son of the man from whom they bought their provisions, arrived with some goats' milk as a present to Glenaladale.

Thus refreshed, they turned their course southwards for Glenmoriston, under their new guide; but they had scarcely gone a mile when Glenaladale missed his purse, which contained the Prince's gold. The Prince found a hiding-place, and Glenaladale and young Borrodale proceeded to search for the purse. They soon found it—empty. There could be no doubt about the thief, for Glenaladale remembered taking it out to give four shillings to the boy who had brought the milk. They walked back to his father's house, and made their complaint. The father seized a rope and threatened to hang the boy to the nearest tree, and the money was returned. The boy's crime saved the Prince. As he lay waiting, with the guide and another attendant, an officer with a small armed party passed close to him, having come by the track along which the fugitives were going. Charles dared not send to warn Glenaladale and his companion, and he lay in grave anxiety until they arrived. The officer had passed them on the other side of a stream, and neither of the two parties had seen the other. If Glenaladale had not missed his purse, and they had all pursued their original route, they must have met the soldiers, and, though they would have outnumbered them, the noise of the conflict could not have failed to bring larger numbers of the enemy.

They went on towards Glenmoriston, walking by night and hiding by day, the Prince made miserable by swarms of midges. On 24th July they reached the Braes of Glenmoriston and found some friendly MacDonalds, Highland robbers by profession, one of whom recognized the Prince. "I hope," he said, "to see you yet in a better condition, as I have seen you before at the head of your army on Glasgow Green." For a week the Prince remained concealed in Glenmoriston. His host told him of a cave which could shelter forty men, the best water in the Highlands running through it, and a heather bed ready for his reception. After three days of these comforts, they moved to another grotto, equally picturesque, but a party of militia was reported to be within four miles of them, and the Prince was again in hopes of finding a French ship at Poolewe.

On the night of 1st August they set out northwards and spent next day in Strathglass, where the Prince rested in a tent made of fir-branches. They continued on this route until 7th August, when, on a hill called Beinn Acharain, they heard again that only one French ship had reached Poolewe, and that it had sailed, leaving behind two French officers who hoped to meet the Prince in the region of Loch Eil. This information led them to retrace their steps, which they did without any adventure until they found themselves again in the Braes of Glenmoriston on 12th August. There they were delayed by a party of soldiers in Glengarry, but the road was soon clear, and they went on without difficulty except for heavy rain and want of provisions. No food could be obtained, for the troops had wasted the country and driven the inhabitants into the hills. But in their utmost need, near Loch Arkaig, one of the party shot a hart, on which they "most deliciously feasted."

On 21st August, on the shores of Loch Arkaig, Archibald Cameron, a brother of Lochiel, who had been a physician in the Prince's army, and was afterwards to give his life for the cause in London, brought to the Prince two French officers who had landed at Poolewe in June, and had been looking for him ever since, but they could give him no information of any value. Two days later, as the Prince lay sleeping, he was told that a party of two hundred men were close to him; a friendly guard was believed to have been placed, and, as they had received no warning, they concluded that there was treachery and that they were surrounded. The Prince asked for his gun, and the small party, eight in number, at once took up a position on the hillside, determined to sell their lives dear. "I was bred a fowler," said Charles. "I can charge quick and am a tolerable marksman, and I can be sure of one at least." But the soldiers, after searching the hut which the Prince had just left, went off in another direction, and Charles lay down and slept peacefully in the rain.

This was his last adventure, for the authorities were giving up the search in despair. Cumberland had left Fort Augustus on 18th July, and his successor as commander-in-chief, the Earl of Albemarle, wrote from Fort Augustus to the Secretary of State on 12th August that he was to leave for Edinburgh next day. "The last party I sent out," he explained "(upon a report that the Pretender's son was in Glen Dessary), returned last night without any tidings of him, and I can make no conjecture of the place he lies concealed in, therefore cannot help suspecting he is gone off, either in some of the small French vessels that have been hovering along the coast, or in a boat to the Long Island. I shall march with the troops, and not leave them till I see them quartered at Perth, Stirling, and other places." On the day the letter was written, the Prince was in Glenmoriston;

three days later, at Loch Arkaig, he was not far from Glen Dessary. He had crossed the head of Glen Dessary on 19th July, and a report to this effect had reached Albemarle much too late. The recall of the troops for their southward march explains the comparative security of the fugitives, and about the same time the militia regiments were disbanded after their fruitless search.

On 27th August MacDonnell of Lochgarry and Dr. Archibald Cameron guided the Prince into the friendly country of Cluny Macpherson, where he was to remain until the arrival of a French ship could be definitely ascertained. Lochiel had a touching meeting with him on 30th August. He knelt to greet his Prince. "No, my dear Lochiel," said Charles, "you don't know who may be looking from the tops of yonder hills." They were entertained in Lochiel's hiding-place, where the fugitive ate minced collops out of a saucepan with a silver spoon and exclaimed that at last he was living like a prince. Cluny himself joined them on 1st September; he had been originally on the side of the Government, but had been captured by the Jacobite army in August 1745, had joined the Prince with his clan after Prestonpans, had marched into England and fought at Falkirk, but had been too late for Culloden. He took the Prince to a cunningly devised refuge which he had provided to avoid the dampness of a cave. Cluny's "cage" was situated in some holly bushes on a rough hillside overlooking Loch Ericht. The floor consisted of rows of felled trees, made level with earth and gravel. Young trees growing between the planks of the floor formed a series of stakes, which served for the construction of a thatched roof bound with ropes made of heather and birch twigs. A large tree which rested on a rock lay across the top of the hut and gave it the appearance of a cage hanging from a tree. A crevice between two stones formed a chimney, and the smoke of the peat fire was so near in colour to the stones that it was invisible. The hut was divided into two chambers, of which the upper was the living room and the lower served as a kitchen.

In this cage, with sentinels posted round, the Prince, with Cluny, Lochiel, Dr. Cameron, and six others, lived pleasantly enough for a week. They had plenty of provisions and found amusement in a pack of cards. At one o'clock in the morning of 13th September, they were roused by a messenger who reported the presence of two French ships in Loch Nan Uamh. No time was to be lost, and they set out at once for the coast of South Morar, but they did not forget to send the news to other fugitives who were in hiding—among them Neil Maceachain, who met them on the coast and escaped with them.

It was still necessary to walk by night and hide by day; but one day the Prince, who had just received three mounted firelocks which he had left in the course of his wanderings, felt himself safe enough to challenge his companions to a test of skill in marksmanship. They threw their bonnets into the air and shot at them, " in which diversion His Royal Highness far exceeded." He played a poor practical joke on one of his followers, wrapping himself in a plaid and lying on the floor of a hut at the entrance to which was a large puddle. As his victim approached, the Prince peeped out of the plaid; and with a cry of " O Lord! my Master! " the unfortunate man fell into the puddle. When they reached the river Lochy, he was greatly delighted by being given some brandy which had been brought from the enemy's garrison at Fort Augustus. On 16th September they reached the ruins of Lochiel's house at Achnacarry, which had been burned by Cumberland, and on the 19th they were once more at Borrodale. Cluny knew that he was safe in his own wild country; and, shortly after midnight, he watched the Prince, with Lochiel and Dr. Archibald Cameron, sail in the frigate *Prince de Conti,* whence they were transferred to her slightly larger consort, *L'Heureux.* The two French vessels had arrived in Loch Boisdale on 5th September; they had been searching for the Prince for a fortnight, and their commanders were beginning to despair of finding him.

All of Prince Charlie's companions who left records of his wanderings testify to his courage and endurance. "The Prince submitted with patience to his adverse fortune, was cheerful, and frequently desired those that were with him to be so. He was cautious when in the greatest danger, never at a loss in resolving what to do. He regretted more the distress of those who suffered for adhering to his interest than the dangers and hardships he was exposed to." If the record of Prince Charlie's escape is honourable to himself, it is not less honourable to the people who, at their gravest peril, sheltered and protected him, and the unforgettable story which clings to Highland glens and island shores speaks not of the Prince alone, but also of the men and women who saved him. Among the things that abide is the memory of such as be faithful in love.

Prince Charlie.

VI

TWO AFRICAN JOURNEYS

In an ancient and closely settled land fateful journeys are for the most part short ones. The key-points of danger and safety are not far apart, and a mile or two may be the margin between success and failure. But in a country of infinite spaces the case is otherwise, and such a country is Africa. Hence African journeys against time have covered wide areas from the days when Moses led the Children of Israel across the Red Sea. They have naturally, too, been associated with seasons of war. In this chapter I propose to tell of two: one taken from the early history of Natal; and the other from the Mashonaland Rebellion, the last of those native wars which seriously threatened the white settlements in the south of the continent.

I

In the thirties of last century South Africa was disturbed by two great movements. One was the rise of the military power of the Zulus, which began when the exiled Dingiswayo, having seen British soldiers in shakos drilling in Cape Town, returned to introduce something of their discipline and drill among his countrymen. His successor, Tchaka, became a kind of black Napoleon, eating up the neighbouring tribes and acquiring their land and cattle, and driving the broken remnants north of the Drakensberg. One of the principal of these refugees, Mosilikatse, fled with his clan north of the Vaal, and became the founder of that Matabele nation which we shall hear of again. After Tchaka came Dingaan, an inferior general, but formidable because he commanded a vigorous nation in arms.

The other movement was caused by the restlessness of the Dutch settlers in Cape Colony under British rule. They disliked the British law which made the black man and the white man equal in legal rights; they objected to taxation; they were offended by many novelties which threatened their old traditions. So some of them took the bold step of moving with their families north into the wilderness, in search of a land where they could live as in the old days.

The story of the Great Trek, a fine story on the whole with many splendid tales in it of heroism against odds, does not concern us here. It suffices to say that, after desperate battles with Mosilikatse, the Boers drove him north of the Limpopo and began the settlement of the countries which we know to-day as the Transvaal and the Orange Free State. Our concern is with the little country of Natal lying to the east of that no-man's-land of Kaffraria, where native wars had been grumbling for thirty years.

Natal is a land of rich valleys lying between the Drakensberg range and the sea. Just after it had been devastated by Tchaka's armies, a small group of British traders arrived at Durban Bay and founded a tiny settlement, which managed to keep on good terms with the Zulu king. In 1834 they petitioned the British Government that the country should be occupied as a British colony, but on financial grounds the British Government declined. Next year appeared a certain Captain Allen Gardiner, an ex-officer of the Royal Navy, who had devoted his life to missionary work. He visited Dingaan's court, but found the soil there unfruitful; so he settled on the coast and was one of the founders of the port of Durban, named in honour of Sir Benjamin D'Urban, the Governor of Cape Colony. Money was raised for clearing the bush and improving the town, and those who had no money to subscribe gave one week's work. Among the latter was a young Englishman, by name Dick King, who acted as Captain Gardiner's wagon driver. Of him we shall presently hear.

When the Great Trek began a party of Boers, under the famous Pieter Uys, trekked through Kaffraria and reached Durban. There they were warmly welcomed by the few British settlers, and on their return to Cape Colony they gave a glowing account of the Promised Land they had discovered. But the main Boer emigration did not take that direction. When the Boers entered Natal in force, they came from the north through the Drakensberg passes under the leadership of Pieter Retief. Retief also received a hearty welcome at Durban, and paid a visit to Dingaan's court in order to arrange for the occupation by his countrymen of some of the land along the Tugela River. The Zulus were purely a nation of soldiers and cattle-owners, and most of the best land in the country was untilled.

The story of the Boers in Natal is one long tragedy. Retief and his company of 200 Boers visited Dingaan's kraal on the 3rd February 1838, and were incontinently massacred. The women and children and the rest of the party were scattered at various points in the Tugela valley, and thither the Zulu regiments of the Black Shields and the White Shields hastened to complete the slaughter. Whole families were butchered, and few indeed were the survivors. The district is still known as Weenen, the "place of weeping," so called by the Boers in memory of a hideous tragedy.

But Dingaan had found an enemy far tougher in

fibre than the Kafir chieftains he had subdued. There were other Boer leaders, who would not rest till they had avenged their countrymen. Two of these, Hendrik Potgeiter and Pieter Uys, who had just defeated Mosilikatse, at once crossed the Drakensberg. The first affair was disastrous, for they were badly beaten. Then the English from Durban attempted a diversion, but they too were defeated by Panda, half-brother to Dingaan, on the Tugela. It looked as if the British settlement was at the mercy of the conqueror, and presently the Zulus were in Durban, looting and destroying, while the settlers had retired to a brig in the bay. They were safe there, however, for every Zulu has a horror of water.

But an avenger was on his way. This was Andries Pretorius, a man of a grim and patient valour, like some Old Testament hero. He raised a new Boer commando, and in November 1838, with 400 men, crossed the Tugela. The Boers held a solemn religious service, and vowed that if the Lord gave them victory they would keep the day of it sacred as a Sabbath in each year. On the 15th December—celebrated ever since by the South African Dutch as Dingaan's Day—Pretorius met the Zulu impis on the banks of the Blood River. The 400 disciplined men, all first-class shots, utterly defeated the black army of many thousands; and when victory was won they showed little mercy to an enemy whom they regarded as accursed of heaven. Among the Boers only three were wounded, while the victors counted over 3,000 Zulu dead. Dingaan fled into the eastern hills, and Pretorius, marching upon the royal kraal, buried the remains of Retief and his companions, which he found bleaching in the sun.

Natal, except for the British settlement on the coast, was now effectively occupied by the Boer emigrants. This raised an awkward problem for Britain and the Cape Government. Under English law a subject of the Crown cannot, by adventuring in the waste places of the earth, acquire sovereignty for himself, but only for his king. The British Government, therefore, could not acknowledge the independent republic which Pretorius and his friends had set up in Natal, and they could not admit that the Boer emigrants, by leaving British territory, had thereby thrown off British allegiance. They therefore resolved to send a small expedition to take possession of Durban and restore order in the country.

In December 1838, Major Charters, with a company of the 72nd Highlanders and three guns, landed there and erected a fort on the Point. While, therefore, Pretorius was breaking Dingaan on the Blood River, the British flag was being hoisted at Durban. Presently Major Charters withdrew, leaving only a small body of troops behind him, under Captain Jervis. Jervis was an honest man, who earnestly desired to arrange a peace between the Zulus and the Boers. This, however, was soon seen to be impossible. The Boer regarded the Zulu as the Israelite regarded the Canaanite, an enemy whom it was his religious duty to extirpate. The British Government withdrew the handful of troops; and no sooner had they gone than the Boers hoisted their own flag on the British flagstaff and proclaimed the Republic of Natalia.

After that the doings of Pretorius and his men became less creditable. Dingaan was unquestionably a brutal and treacherous scoundrel; but the Boers used his own methods against him when they drove him out of the country to exile and death and set up his half-brother Panda in his stead. The truth is that, while many of the leaders of the Great Trek were men of the highest character, a number of common brigands and adventurers made up the tail of the expeditions. The new republic marched from confidence to confidence, and in its relations with Britain showed an arrogance not unnatural perhaps in those who had fought so stubborn a battle.

Presently came a crisis. Some of the Kafir tribes whom Tchaka and Dingaan had expelled began to drift back to Natal, and the Boers, denying all right in the land to its former masters, resolved to settle them in a district south of the Natal border, in what is now the province of Pondoland. There lived a chief called Faku, who, to his surprise, was suddenly attacked by a Boer commando and lost 150 of his men and 3,000 of his cattle. He complained to the Wesleyan missionaries who had settled under his protection, and they forwarded a complaint to the Government of Cape Colony. The situation had become serious, for it looked as if the Boers in Natal were about to set a spark to the powder magazine of Kaffraria, the dangers of which Cape Colony knew only too well. Accordingly a small British force of 250 men, under Captain Smith, was ordered to march to Durban. He arrived in Natal in March 1842, and without interference took possession of the fort on the Point and pitched his camp outside the town about half a mile from the sea.

Pretorius and his men instantly challenged his authority, and presently the little force was besieged. Captain Smith resolved to make a night attack on the Boer headquarters ; but the English regulars proved less adroit than the Boer sharpshooters and were driven back with considerable losses. A short truce was arranged to bury the dead ; and it became very clear that unless relief came at once the British would soon be driven into the sea.

The difficulty was to get news of the situation to the British authorities. It was impossible to send by water, and 600 miles of savage country lay between Durban and the first Cape Colony settlement of Grahamstown. That country was Kaffraria, full of angry native tribes, bitterly hostile to the Boers, and for the most part scarcely less hostile to the British. Moreover, the Boer lines lay around the town, and it might be no easy task to pass them. But Grahamstown was the only hope, and volunteers were asked for to make the perilous journey. Dick King, the man whom we have seen as Captain Gardiner's wagoner, responded. He was a man of wiry physique, sound veldcraft, and above all he had mixed much with the Kafirs and knew most of their tongues. Two of the best troop horses in Captain Smith's force were selected, and in the evening were rowed across Durban Bay.

Such is the sequence of events which led to Dick King's great ride. When he was ferried over the twilit waters of the bay he was engaged on an errand even more fateful than he thought. He believed that he was only doing a brave man's part in getting help for sorely tried comrades; but in truth he was settling the fate of the colony of Natal. The British Government at home were averse to any expansion of territory, and above all averse to becoming involved in a war. Had the stockade at Durban fallen, in all likelihood they would have done nothing further, but made terms with Pretorius and recognized his republic. That would have meant that Natal would have developed as a Dutch state instead of being the most purely English colony in South Africa. The fate of the little country was involved in one man's ride.

King's task seemed in the last degree impossible. There was no chance of getting fresh mounts, so he must ride each horse in turn and lead the other, and somehow nurse the two beasts over 600 miles. The country was for the most part grassy down-land, broken by rocky ridges and furrowed by deep rivers descending from the Drakensberg. Over these rivers there were no bridges and few fords. There were no roads, only native tracks. All the tribes were suspicious and most of them hostile. Above all there was desperate need for haste, and a man in a hurry must go blindly. He has no time to make wide circuits and take proper precautions for secrecy.

Before daybreak King had crossed the Umkomangi River and was well started. For food he had to trust to mealie-pap at Kafir kraals, and that meant he must keep on the good side of the different tribes he met. Two advantages he had—his complete knowledge of their speech, and the fact that scattered among them were various Wesleyan missionaries who might be trusted to befriend him. He was also on the side which, on the whole, they favoured, for memories of Pretorius's raid on Faku were still bitter in the countryside. Probably no living man but he could have made the journey, and as it fell out he had little trouble with the Kafirs. The Amabaka tribe did, indeed, take him prisoner under the belief that he was a Boer; but when they found that he was British they at once released him.

His main difficulties were the pathless country and the great distance. Wild animals, which have now been driven into the far north, were then as thick in the countryside as they are to-day in a game preserve. Elephants roamed in the patches of forest; there were lions in every thicket; and the African buffalo, almost the most dangerous of African beasts, filled the river marshes. To an old hunter, however, wild beasts are the least of perils in the bush, for they will rarely attack one who appears to have no hostile purpose. But the rivers were full with the rains from the hills, and he had to swim them from bank to bank. Also it was no light task, even for an old hunter, to find his way in a pathless land, where a false turn might lead him into impenetrable marshes or jungles where every yard had to be fought for.

Poor food and excessive fatigue soon began to tell upon his strength. In a ride against time a man's nerves are highly strung, and this adds greatly to the

He and his two horses did an average of not less than eighty miles a day.

See page 122.

physical burden. About the third day he began to suffer from chill and fever, and the wait-a-bit thorns and prickly-pear scrub began to dance before his eyes. Every one who has ridden through the African bush with fever on him knows the misery of the experience —the blinding headache, the unbearable thirst, the shivering fits which make it difficult to keep in the saddle. King forced his body to its utmost limits; but he was compelled every now and then to lie down and rest. One or two missionaries whom he encountered doctored him as best they could; but altogether the better part of two days was wasted in bouts of illness.

Nevertheless the iron spirit of the man prevailed. Allowing for the delays caused by illness, he and his two horses did an average of not less than eighty miles a day. On the ninth day after leaving Durban he stumbled into the little settlement of Grahamstown, half blinded with fatigue and fever, but able to give the message which was to save his comrades.

Colonel Hare, Lieutenant-Governor of the Eastern Province, was not a man to waste time. He at once ordered the Grenadier company of the 27th Regiment to proceed from Port Elizabeth to Durban, and Sir George Napier immediately afterwards sent the 25th Regiment from the Cape. Exactly one month from King's start, a British ship carrying reinforcements sailed into Durban Bay and found the British flag still flying. Dick King's wild ride had not been in vain.

II

In March 1896 a grave native rebellion broke out in Matabeleland, the south-western portion of the then new colony of Rhodesia. A rebellion of some sort was almost inevitable. Though their chief, Lobengula, had been defeated, the Matabele people had never been really conquered; and as white civilization and white settlement began to spread throughout the country it was certain that a warlike race would not accept the overthrow of their old life without a further struggle. Three months later the rebellion spread to the north-western province of Mashonaland, and there the number of independent and isolated tribes made the task of suppression more difficult. The chief town of Mashonaland is Salisbury, but scattered in the country round were a number of embryo townships connected by precarious roads. Everywhere there was a large native population, and the white residents were separated by many miles of difficult country from their fellows.

The first threat of trouble in Mashonaland began in the Hartley Hill district to the south-west of Salisbury. As always happens with native risings, it spread rapidly to districts hundreds of miles distant. About 14th June Salisbury was thoroughly alarmed, and provision was made for its defence. It was an extremely scattered town, and the outlying houses had to be relinquished and the whole population brought into a central laager. On the night of the 18th the homestead of the Vicomtesse de la Panouse, two miles from the town, was visited by a party of rebels. The Vicomtesse only escaped by hiding in the grass and creeping into Salisbury under cover of night.

Our story begins a week later, on the highroad which ran from Salisbury to Umtali on the Portuguese border. Along this road were various stores and settlements, the chief being at a place called Marandellas, some forty or fifty miles down the road. On the morning of 16th June Miss Carter, a Salisbury lady, left Salisbury for Umtali in a passenger wagon, accompanied by Mr. Lamb, three other white men, two natives, and a Cape driver. On the 18th the down coach for Umtali passed them, but the driver had no news to give them of the troubles which were then beginning on the other side of Salisbury.

When they reached Marandellas they found the Vicomte de la Panouse with a party and a large wagon laden with stores. They also received a note from the station of Headlands, some twenty miles on, urging them to return to Salisbury, as the Mashonas were everywhere rising. At first they were inclined to disregard the warning. But they returned to Marandellas, where they received another message begging them to waste no time in getting back. Again they hesitated, for Marandellas seemed a very safe retreat, since it held a large supply of ammunition. Discretion, however, prevailed, and they moved out on the Salisbury road, where they overtook the Vicomte de la Panouse and his party. It was resolved that they would travel back together, for the Vicomte had with him three white men, and there was also an ox-wagon with several attendants anxious to join in the convoy.

The Vicomte's wagon, which was drawn by donkeys and was very heavily laden, moved slowly, and it was not till the afternoon of the following day that it reached the store of Messrs. Graham and White. Here they realized for the first time their imminent danger. All the native boys had gone, and one who had crawled through to warn Mr. Graham had had a hard fight and was badly wounded. The party made a laager round the store, and the night passed peacefully. Next morning they begged Mr. Graham to accompany them to Salisbury. He refused, however, believing that he was quite able to hold the place. The following day he was attacked and murdered as he was escaping into the veld.

That Monday morning, after leaving Mr. Graham's store, the sentry whom they had placed on the top of Mr. Lamb's wagon pointed out several black forms in the distance. The wagons moved peacefully along for some six miles, and then outspanned for the midday rest. By this time their field-glasses showed the party large numbers of natives massing, all of whom seemed to be armed. After that the wagons kept close together. When they had gone another mile they came upon a horrible sight. Lying in the road were three mutilated bodies, which proved to be those of a store-keeper, Mr. Weyer, his wife, and his child; a little farther on lay the body of another child hideously maltreated. As the twilight was approaching there was no time to bury the dead, and all that could be done was to place the poor remains together and to cover them with sand and some branches of trees. The bodies were all in sleeping garments, so it seemed that they had been murdered during the past night when trying to escape.

This grim sight, seen in the bright South African twilight, brought awe into the hearts of the little band. Darkness was falling; all round them was the thick bushveld. The Vicomte's wagon was heavily laden and could only move slowly, and all the animals were tired. The Vicomte lightened his load by flinging away some of his goods, and they had barely resumed their journey when, looking back, they saw a large body of natives carrying off the abandoned flour. Mr. Lamb climbed to the top of his wagon, and had the satisfaction of seeing one fall to his rifle. The enemy returned the fire, wounding one of the donkeys.

It was now fairly clear that unless they could move faster the whole convoy was doomed, so it became necessary to jettison the whole wagon load. The Vicomte did this unwillingly, but there was no other course. His donkeys were unharnessed and driven on in front; the other wagon was also left derelict, and the oxen from it inspanned in front of Mr. Lamb's donkeys. Behind them they could hear loud shouts as the rebels looted the discarded wagons.

Suddenly fire was opened upon them from the bushes on the right hand, and a brisk exchange of shots took place. It was now very dark, and as they crawled along the road a perpetual fusillade was kept up. Happily they had several good dogs with them, who were sent into the roadside bush and so gave early notice of an ambuscade. Presently the enemy fire died away; the moon came out, and at a better pace the convoy reached Law's Store.

It was now about 11 p.m. They found the place deserted and looted; but it was possible to make of it some kind of protection for the night. A few outer huts were burnt in order to give a field of fire; the animals were secured in a laager, and the party took refuge in one of the rooms. Pickets were posted, three at a time in two watches. The Cape boys lit fires before and behind the house, which were a comfort to the pickets, for the night had the bitter cold of a Rhodesian winter.

At 2 a.m. next morning a Cape boy, badly wounded, crawled up. He had escaped from a neighbouring farm, and had been fighting since 6 a.m. the previous morning. At 4 a.m. all the men of the party went on guard till daybreak. As soon as the first light appeared the convoy started, and they had not gone a mile when, looking back, they saw a huge cloud of smoke ascending from Law's Store. The rebels had closed in behind them and burned the place.

All morning they crept along the road, being fired at from every patch of bush. One shot passed between the Vicomte and Mr. Lamb, killing a dog as it walked between them; another passed through the side of the passenger wagon in front of Miss Carter, and then below the armpit of one of the Cape boys. These Cape boys, let it be said, showed throughout this adventure, and throughout the whole rebellion, the utmost courage and fidelity.

No one of the party believed at this time that they would ever arrive at Salisbury. The next station on the road was a place called Ballyhooley, and just before reaching it they had a serious fight, where one of the Cape boys managed to shoot the rebel leader. Ballyhooley they found deserted and looted. There they had hoped to meet relief parties from Salisbury; but none were there, and the passenger wagon, drawn by its donkeys and oxen, crawled on again, the men tramping alongside in the dust. At every turn of the road, and in every patch of scrub, they feared to meet their fate.

They were now only three miles from the town, when to their horror they saw a large number of rebels massed together. For a little they had a terrible fear that Salisbury might have fallen. But fatigue and anxiety had by now dulled their senses, and they had mercifully ceased to realize their peril. They stopped for a little to allow the Cape boys to detach the oxen from the wagon, so that they might be turned loose, and while they did so a crowd of natives swarmed on the kopjes above them. Then they moved on, and as they emerged from the hills they came in sight of Salisbury, which seemed to be a town of the dead.

But suddenly in the middle distance they observed three or four mounted men galloping towards them. They saw that they were friends, and presently they realized that the defences of Salisbury were still intact, and that at last they had found sanctuary.

The little party had come out of the very jaws of death. Behind and around them for three days had been the enemy, flushed with success, confident that the days of the white man in the land were numbered; every little storehouse and farmstead was in ruins, every inn was a heap of charred timbers and burned stores and broken bottles. They had to move at the slow pace set by tired oxen and donkeys. The odds were all against them when they left Marandellas, and they won through only by virtue of that tenacity of spirit which obstinately refuses to despair.

Charles I.

VII

THE GREAT MONTROSE

THE story of the paladin of Scottish history, the man whom Cardinal de Retz thought equal to any of the heroes of antiquity, is scarcely to be equalled for swift drama in the records of any land. James Graham, the first Marquis of Montrose, began his marvellous career at the age of thirty-two, and crowded into two years the campaigns which made him master of Scotland. He died on the scaffold when he was only thirty-eight, leaving behind him the reputation of perhaps the greatest soldier ever born north of the Tweed, and certainly one of the purest and most chivalrous figures in his country's annals. Few men have ever covered country with his lightning speed, and the whole tale of his exploits is a tale of escapes and hurried journeys. I propose to tell of two episodes in his short career, but I would add that they are no more stirring than a dozen others.

I

In 1642 the English Civil War began. Sir John Hotham shut the gates of Hull in the King's face. On the 22nd of August Charles raised the Royal Standard at Nottingham, and on 22nd October was fought the Battle of Edgehill. Montrose had originally been a

Covenanter—that is, he had signed the National Covenant which protested against the imposition of a foreign church system on Scotland. He commanded an army in the first Covenant War, but as time went on he began to see that more was involved in the struggle than the question of liturgies. He realized that the Church in Scotland was beginning to make claims which meant the complete abolition of civil government. He therefore drew towards the King's side, and there began that antagonism with the Marquis of Argyll which was inevitable between two men with such different temperaments and creeds.

In the early winter of 1643 he joined the King's court at Oxford, and proposed to Charles "to raise Scotland" on his behalf. It looked a crazy proposal, for even then the Scottish army was over the Border in arms against the King, and the Covenant held every city north of the Tweed. The few loyalists who still stood out were mostly vain nobles who had some personal quarrel with the other side. But such was the ardour of the young Montrose that he impressed the King and his graver councillors like Hyde and Endymion Porter. He asked for little help. Lord Antrim was to raise troops in Ireland and land in the west of Scotland to keep Argyll occupied in his own country. Montrose himself hoped to borrow a body of horse from Newcastle's army in the north to help him to cut his way through the Lowlands to the Highland line. Charles consented, and Antrim was sent to Ulster, with instructions to land 2,000 troops in Argyll by April 1, 1644. Montrose was made lieutenant-general of the King's forces in Scotland, and on a March morning in 1644 he left Oxford by the north road to win a kingdom for his master.

When St. Theresa, as a child, set out to convert the Moors, she was engaged in an adventure scarcely less hopeful than that which Montrose had now set himself. Where was he to find troops? The best of the old professional soldiers were with Leven. He could get nothing in the Scottish Lowlands, for on them the Kirk had laid an iron hand. The nobles and the gentry were jealous and self-centred. Antrim's Ulstermen would do more harm than good; for though most of them were Scots and Macdonalds, they were Catholics and would drive every Presbyterian to the other side. There was no solid hope anywhere save in the soul of the adventurer. He flung himself into a hostile country without a base, without troops, without munitions, in the hope that his fiery spirit would create armies out of nothing.

He reached Newcastle's camp safely and found that things there were going badly. Newcastle could only offer him 100 ill-mounted troopers and two brass cannon—a poor outfit for the conquest of Scotland. He managed to raise some of the northern militia and a band of local gentlemen, and with 1,300 men he crossed the Border in April and took Dumfries. There, however, he could not stay. The gentry of Nithsdale and Annandale would not stir, and he was compelled to return to England, where he found that Newcastle had flung himself into York and was closely beset by Leven, Fairfax, and Manchester. With a handful of men he captured Morpeth, and presently he received a summons from Prince Rupert, who was then marching through Lancashire to the relief of York. He set off to join him, but before they met the King's cause had suffered its first disaster. Rupert indeed relieved York; but on the 2nd July, about five in the afternoon, he met the Parliamentary forces on Marston Moor and discovered that new thing in England—the shock of Cromwell's horse. His army was scattered; Newcastle fled overseas; and he himself, with some 6,000 troops, rode westward into Wales. Two days after the battle Montrose found him in an inn at Richmond, in Yorkshire; but Rupert had nothing to give. On the contrary, he stood much in need of Montrose's scanty recruits. So with a sad heart Montrose rode by Brough and Appleby to Carlisle, to write his report of failure to the King.

Four months had passed and nothing had been achieved. The news from Scotland was the worst conceivable. The land lay quiet under the Covenant, and Antrim's levies seemed to have vanished into the air. The nobles were tumbling over each other in their anxiety to swear fealty to Argyll. There seemed nothing to be done except to surrender the royal commission and go abroad to wait for happier times. So his friends advised, and Montrose made a pretence of acquiescing. He set out for the south with his friends, but a mile out of Carlisle he slipped behind, and, as his servants and baggage went on, it was presumed that he was following. It was as well that he stopped, for the rest of the party were captured by Fairfax at Ribble Bridge.

He had resolved on the craziest of adventures. He would break through the Covenanting cordon in the Lowlands and win to his own country of Perthshire, where lived his kinsmen. There, at any rate, were loyal hearts, and something might be devised to turn the tide. He chose as his companions Sir William Rollo, who was lame, and Colonel Sibbald, who had served under him before. These two wore the dress of Leven's troopers, while Montrose followed behind as their groom, riding one ill-conditioned horse and leading another.

It was a dangerous road to travel. The country was strewn with broken men and patrolled by Covenanting dragoons, and a gentleman in those days was not so easily disguised. At first all went smoothly. The disreputable clan of the Grahams held the lower Esk, and as the three rode through the woods of Netherby they learned that its chief, Sir Richard Graham, had joined the Covenant and appointed himself Warden of the Marches. This they had from one of his servants, who spoke freely to them as to Leven's troopers. A little farther on they fell in with a Scot, one of Newcastle's soldiers, who, to their consternation, disregarded Rollo and Sibbald, but paid great attention to the groom and hailed him by his proper title. Montrose tried to deny it; but the man exclaimed, "What! do I not know my Lord Marquis of Montrose well enough? Go your way and God be with you." A gold piece rewarded the untimely well-wisher.

The journey grew daily more anxious till the Forth was passed. "It may be thought," says Patrick Gordon, a Royalist historian, "that God Almighty sent His good angel to lead the way, for he went, as if a cloud had environed him, through all his enemies." We do not know the exact route they travelled, whether by Annandale and then by Tweed or Clyde, or up Eskdale and thence over the Tweedside range to the Lothians. Probably they went by the former, and followed the belt of moorland which runs north by Carnwath almost to the Highland hills. From Carlisle to Perth is a hundred miles, and the party rode by day and night, keeping, we may suppose, away from towns and villages and frequented parts of the highway.

On the fourth day they came to the Montrose lands in Stirling and Strathearn, but they did not draw rein till they reached the house of Tullibelton between Perth and Dunkeld. Here lived Patrick Graham of Inchbrakie, one of the best loved of all Montrose's kin, and here at any rate was safe shelter for the traveller while he spied out the land and looked about for an army.

So the curtain rises, and the first act of the great drama reveals a forlorn little party late on an August evening knocking at the door of a woodland tower about the shining reaches of Tay. The King's lieutenant-general makes a very modest entry on the scene. Two followers, four sorry screws, little money, and no baggage, seem a slender outfit for the conquest of a kingdom; but in six months he was to see Scotland at his feet.

For six days the royal lieutenant lay in close hiding, spending most of his time in the woods and hollows, sleeping at night in hunters' bothies. The scouts he had sent out returned with a melancholy tale. Huntly in the north had made a mess of it, and the Gordons were leaderless and divided. Even some of the Graham and Drummond kinsmen were in arms against the King. There were rumours of a Covenant army in Aberdeenshire, and Argyll in the west had his clan in arms. Montrose wondered at this strange activity. The battleground now was England, and, with Scotland in so iron a grip, these elaborate military precautions seemed needless.

He was soon to learn the reason. As he was one day in the wood of Methven, sleeping the night there, he fell into a great despondency of spirit. While he reflected upon the hopelessness of his case, he suddenly saw a man carrying a fiery cross and making for the town of Perth. He stopped him and inquired what the matter was. The messenger told him that Alastair MacDonald of Ulster, commonly called Colkitto (a corruption of the Gaelic word meaning "Coll who can fight with either hand"), had come into Atholl with a great army of Irish. At last Antrim's levies had come out of the mist. Presently Montrose had a letter from Alastair MacDonald himself, directed to him at Carlisle, announcing his arrival and asking for instructions.

If Montrose needed help, no less did the Irish commander. He had landed in July in Ardnamurchan, on the west coast, and proceeded to ravage the Campbell lands. His ships were all destroyed, so he resolved, being in a desperate situation, to march across Scotland and join the Gordons. But in Lochaber he heard that the Gordons had made their peace with the

Covenant, and the other northern clans, like the Mackenzies, had no love for Alastair's tartan and would have nothing to do with him. Headed back on all sides, Alastair decided that the boldest course was the safest. He marched to the head-waters of the Spey and issued a summons calling on the clans to rise in the names of the King and Huntly. This brought him 500 recruits, most of them Gordons; but the other clans refused and blocked the road down the Spey.

He now seemed in a fair way to be exterminated. The Campbells intercepted his retreat to the sea, and Argyll was hot-foot on his track. The Mackenzies cut him off from the north and east, his new levies were mutinous and distrustful, and south lay the unfriendly Lowlands and clans like the Stewarts of Atholl, who would never serve under any leader of an alien name. He had proved that, whoever might band the Highlands into an army, it would not be a man of Highland blood. Hence his despairing letter to the lieutenant-general asking for instructions and help. He can scarcely have hoped for much from his appeal, for Carlisle was a long way from Badenoch and he had the enemy on every side.

Montrose sent an answer, bidding Alastair be of good heart and await him at Blair. The latter obeyed and marched into Atholl, but the local clans resented his appearance. The fiery cross was sent round, and there seemed every chance of a desperate conflict between two forces who alike detested the Covenant and followed the King.

The situation was saved by a hairbreadth. Montrose, accompanied by Patrick Graham the younger of Inchbrakie—Black Pate, as the countryside called him—set off on foot over the hills to keep the tryst. He had acquired from Inchbrakie a Highland dress—the trews, a short coat, and a plaid round his shoulders. He wore, we are told, a blue bonnet with a bunch of oats as a badge, and he carried a broadsword and a Highland buckler. Thus accoutred he entered upon the scene in the true manner of romance, unlooked-for and invincible.

Alastair and his ragged troops were waiting hourly on battle, when across the moor they saw two figures advancing. Black Pate was known to every Atholl man, and there were many who had seen Montrose. Loud shouts of welcome apprised the Ulsterman that here was no bonnet laird, but when he heard that it was indeed the King's lieutenant he could scarcely believe his ears. He had looked for cavalry, an imposing bodyguard, and a figure more like his own swashbuckling self than this slim young man with the quiet face and searching grey eyes.

In a moment all quarrels were forgotten. Montrose produced his commission and Alastair promptly took service under him, thankful to be out of a plight which for weeks had looked hopeless. The Atholl Highlanders were carried off their feet by the grace and fire of their new leader, and 800 of them brought to his side those broadswords which that morning had been dedicated to cutting Ulster throats. Next morning the Royal Standard was unfurled on a green knoll above the river Tilt. The King's lieutenant had got him an army.

II

I pass over the next two months. On the 1st September, with his ill-assorted forces, he met the Covenant army under Lord Elcho at Tippermuir, near Perth, and scattered it to the winds. Then he marched to Aberdeen, and on the 13th of that month soundly defeated another army under Lord Balfour of Burleigh. Thereafter his difficulties increased. He found that his Lowland gentlemen began to slip away, for they had no love for a mid-winter campaign conducted

Across the moor they saw
two figures advancing.

See page 136.

at Montrose's incredible pace. Moreover, Alastair went off on an expedition of his own to the west, and the rest of the Highlanders had private grievances, the avenging of which they thought of far greater moment than any royal necessities.

The end of November came; the heavy rains in the glens told of the beginning of winter, and the hills were whitened with snow. Argyll was at Dunkeld, and for a moment the campaign languished. Then one morning at Blair, Alastair's pipes announced his return, bringing with him the rest of his Ulstermen and a considerable levy of the western clans—MacDonalds of Glengarry, Keppoch, and Clanranald, Macleans from Morvern and Mull, Stewarts from Appin, and Camerons from Lochaber. The clans had only one object, to take order with Argyll, for they hated the house of Diarmaid far more than the Covenant. Now was the time to avenge ancient wrongs and to break the pride of a chief who had boasted that no mortal enemy could enter his country. The hour had come when the fray must be carried to Lorn.

Montrose had that supreme virtue in a commander which recognizes facts. He could not maintain his army without war, and Lowland war they would not as yet listen to. If he looked to their help in the future he must whet their valour and rivet their loyalty by fresh successes. In return for their assistance in the King's quarrel they must have the help of the King's lieutenant in their own. Besides, the plan could be justified on other grounds of strategy and politics. A blow at the Campbells in their own country would shatter Argyll's not too robust nerve, and put fear into the heart of the Covenant.

But it was the wildest of wild adventures. Clan Campbell was the largest, most prosperous, and most civilized of all the Highland peoples. Indeed, they formed almost a separate state, and it was not without reason that Argyll had boasted that his land was impregnable. Strategically it had every advantage. On the eastern side, where it looked to the Lowlands, there were the castles of Roseneath and Dunoon to keep watch, and deep sea lochs to hinder the invader. South and west lay the sea, and the Campbells had what little navy existed in Scotland at the time. North lay a land of high mountains and difficult passes, where no man could travel save by permission of the sovereign lord. Moreover, the Campbells of Lochow and Glenorchy had flung their tentacles over Breadalbane and held the glens around the head-waters of Tay. There might be a raid of Macgregors or Maclarens on the east, or a foray from Appin on Loch Etive side, but it seemed that not even the King and his army could get much beyond the gates. "It is a far cry to Lochow," so ran the Campbell watchword, and it was a farther cry to Inveraray.

When Montrose assented to Alastair's wishes he resolved to strike straight at the enemy's heart. He would wage war not on the outskirts but in the citadel. Through Breadalbane ran a possible route among wild glens and trackless bogs, which at this winter season would be deep in snow. This was the old raiding road out of Lorn, and Argyll flattered himself that his clan alone had the keys of it. But with Montrose were men who had made many a midnight foray into the Campbell country, and who knew every corrie and scaur as well as any son of Diarmaid. A Glencoe man, Angus MacAlain Dubh, is named by tradition as the chief guide, and he promised Montrose that his army could live well on the country, "if tight houses, fat cattle, and clear water will suffice."

From Blair, past the shores of Loch Tay swept the advance till the confines of Breadalbane were reached and a country that owned Campbell sway. Up Glen Dochart they went, following much the same road as the present railway line to Oban, past Crianlarich and Tyndrum, and into the glens of Orchy. It was a raid of vengeance, and behind them rose the flames of burning roof-trees. Presently Loch Awe lay before them under a leaden winter sky, and soon the little peels of the lochside lairds smoked to heaven. It was a cruel business, save that the women and children were spared. All fighting men were slain or driven to the high hills, every cot and clachan was set alight, and rows of maddened cattle attested the richness of the land and the profit of the invaders. It was Highland warfare of the old barbarous type, no worse and no better than that which Argyll had already carried to Lochaber and Badenoch and the Braes of Angus.

Argyll was well served by his scouts, and to him at Edinburgh word was soon brought of Montrose's march to Breadalbane. He must have thought it a crazy venture; now at last was his enemy delivered into his hands. No human army could cross the winter passes even if it had the key; and the men of Glenorchy would wipe out the starving remnants at their leisure. Full of confidence he posted across Scotland to Inveraray. There he found that all was quiet. Rumours of a foray in Lorn were indeed rife, but the burghers of Inveraray, strong in their generations of peace, had no fear for themselves. Argyll saw to the defences of the castle, and called a great gathering of the neighbouring clansmen to provide reinforcements, if such should be needed, for the Glenorchy and Breadalbane men, who by this time had assuredly made an end of Montrose.

Suddenly came a thunderbolt. Wild-eyed shepherds rushed into the streets with the cry that the MacDonalds were upon them. Quickly the tale flew. Montrose was not in Breadalbane or on the fringes of Lorn. He was at Loch Awe—nay, he was in the heart of Argyll itself. The chief waited no longer. He found a fishing boat, and, the wind being right, fled down Loch Fyne to the shelter of his castle at Roseneath. The same breeze that filled his sails brought the sound of Alastair's pipes, and he was scarcely under weigh ere the van of the invaders came down Glen Shira.

Then began the harrying of Clan Campbell. Leaderless and unprepared, they made no resistance to Montrose's army of flushed and battle-worn warriors. Macleans and MacDonalds, Stewarts and Camerons, satiated their ancient grudges with the plunder of Inveraray. The kerns thawed their half-frozen limbs at the warmth of blazing steadings, and appeased their ravenous hunger at the expense of the bakers and vintners and fleshers of the burgh. Never had the broken men of Lochaber and the Isles fared so nobly. For some happy weeks they ran riot in what for them was a land of milk and honey, while the townsmen, crouching in cellars and thickets, or safe behind the castle gates, wondered how long it would be before their chief returned to avenge them. There seems to have been no special barbarity about the business. Here and there a refractory Campbell was dirked, but Alastair's men preferred victual and cattle to human blood.

Meantime word had gone from the exile at Roseneath to the Government in Edinburgh. It was for Argyll to avenge the shame of his clan, and he presently received 1,100 of the flower of the Scottish militia. His kinsman, Sir Duncan Campbell of Auchinbreck, was summoned back from Ireland. Seaforth was waiting with a northern army at Inverness, and the Scottish commander-in-chief, William Baillie of Letham, was at Perth. It looked as if Montrose had walked into a certain trap. He would be caught between Argyll and Seaforth, and if he tried to escape to the right Baillie would await him. It seemed the certainty on which Argyll loved to gamble.

Mid-winter that year was open and mild. Had it been otherwise Clan Campbell must have been annihilated and Montrose could never have led his men safely out of Argyll. About the middle of January 1645 he gave orders for the march. He had as yet no news of Argyll's preparations, but he must have realized that the avenger would not be slow on his track. His immediate intention was to come to an account with Seaforth, who not only barred him from the Gordon country but was responsible for the opposition of the powerful clan of Mackenzie. He had guides who promised to show him an easy way out of Lorn into Lochaber. After that his road ran straight up the Great Glen to Inverness.

Laden with miscellaneous plunder and cumbered no doubt with *spreaghs* of cattle, the Highlanders crossed from Loch Awe to the shore of Loch Etive. Since they had nothing to fear in front of them, they continued up the steep brink of that loch to the site of the present house of Glen Etive. Crossing the *beallach* by the old drove-road, they marched through Appin and up Glencoe to the neighbourhood of Corrour, for the shorter road by Kingshouse and the Moor of Rannoch was no place for a heavily laden force in mid-winter. From Corrour the road was that now taken by the West Highland Railway. Passing Loch Treig they descended the valley of the Spean to the shores of Loch Lochy and the opening of the Great Glen. By the evening of Thursday, the 30th January, Montrose was at Kilcumin at the head of Loch Ness. Most of the Atholl men and the bulk of Clanranald had left him, after their custom, to deposit their booty. No more than 1,500 remained—Alastair's Irish, a handful of Stewarts, Macleans, and Camerons, and sufficient cavalry to mount the Lowland gentry and provide an escort for the Standard.

At Kilcumin Montrose had definite news of Seaforth. He was thirty miles off at Inverness with 5,000 men—Frasers, Mackenzies, and regulars from the Inverness garrison. Montrose was preparing to make short work of Seaforth when he received graver tidings. Ian Lom

MacDonald, the bard of Keppoch, arrived to tell of Argyll at his heels. The Campbells were only thirty miles behind at Inverlochy, 3,000 men-at-arms eager to avenge the wrongs of Lorn. They were burning and harrying Glen Spean and Glen Roy and the Lochaber braes, and their object was to take Montrose in the rear what time Seaforth should hold him in the front.

The plight of the little army seemed hopeless; 1,500 very weary men were caught between two forces of 3,000 and 5,000. There was no way of escape to west or east, for the one would lead them to a bare seacoast and the other into the arms of Baillie's foot. Of the two hostile forces the Campbells were the more formidable. Montrose knew very well that the fighting spirit of Clan Diarmaid was equal to any in the Highlands, and now that they were commanded by a skilled soldier and infuriated by the burning of their homes, he could scarcely hope to fight them at long odds. But it is the duty of a good general when he is confronted by two immediate perils to meet the greater first. Montrose resolved to fight the Campbells, but to fight them in his own way.

Early on the morning of Friday, 31st January, began that flank march which remains one of the great exploits in the history of British arms. The little river Tarff flows from the Monadliadh Mountains to Loch Ness. Up its rocky course went Montrose, and the royal army disappeared into the hills. Scouts of Argyll or Seaforth who traversed the Great Glen on that day must have reported no enemy. From Tarff Montrose crossed the pass to Glen Turritt, and, following it downwards, reached Glen Roy. Pushing on through the night, he came to the Bridge of Roy, where that stream enters the Spean, on the morning of Saturday, 1st February. The weather had been bitterly cold, the upper glens were choked with snowdrifts, and the army had neither food nor fire. The road led through places where great avalanches yawned above the adventurers, and over passes so steep and narrow that a hundred men could have held an army at bay. As they struggled along at the pace of a deerstalker, Montrose walked by his men, shaming them to endurance by the spectacle of his own courage. If the reader wishes for a picture of that miraculous march he will find it in the words of young Elrigmore in Mr. Neil Munro's *John Splendid* :—

> " It was like some hyperborean hell, and we the doomed wretches sentenced to our eternity of toil. We had to climb up the shoulder of the hill, now among tremendous rocks, now through water unfrozen, now upon wind-swept ice, but the snow —the snow—the heartless snow—was our constant companion. It stood in walls before, it lay in ramparts round us, it wearied the eye to a most numbing pain. Unlucky were they who wore trews, for the same clung damply to knee and haunch and froze, while the stinging sleet might flay the naked limb till the blood rose among the pelt of the kilted, but the suppleness of the joint was unmarred. . . . At the head of Glen Roy the MacDonalds, who had lost their bauchles of brogues in the pass, started to a trot, and as the necessity was we had to take up the pace too. Long lank hounds, they took the road like deer, their limbs purple with the cold, their faces pinched to the aspect of the wolf, their targets and muskets clattering about them. ' There are Campbells to slay, and suppers to eat,' the major-general had said ; and it would have given the most spiritless followers the pith to run till morning across a strand of rock and pebble. They knew no tiring, they seemingly felt no pain in their torn and bleeding feet, but put mile after mile below them."

From Roy bridge to Inverlochy is some thirteen miles, but to take Argyll in the flank a circuit was necessary, and Montrose followed the northern slopes of the wild tangle of mountains, the highest in Britain, that surround Ben Nevis. In the ruddy gloaming of the February day the vanguard saw beneath and before them the towers of Inverlochy, "like a scowl on the fringe of the wave," and not a mile off the men of Clan Diarmaid making ready their evening meal. Shots were exchanged with the pickets, but no effort was made to advance. Montrose waited quietly in the gathering dusk till by eight o'clock the rest of his famished column had arrived. There, supperless and cold, they passed the night, keeping up a desultory skirmishing with the Campbell outposts, for Montrose was in dread lest Argyll should try to escape. It was a full moon, and the dark masses of both armies were visible to each other. Argyll thought the forces he saw were only a contingent of Highland raiders under Keppoch or some petty chief. But after his fashion he ran no personal risks; so, with his favourite minister and one or two Edinburgh bailies, he withdrew to a boat on Loch Eil.

At dawn on Candlemas day his ears were greeted by an unwelcome note. It was no bagpipe such as Keppoch might use, but trumpets of war, and the salute they sounded was that reserved for the Royal Standard. The King's lieutenant, who two days ago was for certain at Loch Ness, had by some craft of darkness taken wings and flown his army over the winter hills. There was no alternative but to fight. Till Montrose was beaten the Campbells could neither march forward to join Seaforth nor backward to their own land.

Auchinbreck drew up his forces with the fighting men of Clan Campbell in the centre and the Lowland regiments borrowed from Baillie on each wing. Montrose himself led the Royalist centre, with Alastair on the left and Alastair's lieutenant, O'Kean, on the right. Sir Thomas Ogilvy commanded the little troop of horse which had managed to make its way with the infantry over the terrible hills. This was the one advantage Montrose possessed. Otherwise his men were on the point of starvation, having had scarcely a mouthful for forty-eight hours. He himself and Lord Airlie breakfasted on a little raw meal mixed with cold water, which they ate with their dirks.

The battle began with a movement by Ogilvy's horse, which gravely disquieted the Lowland wings. Then the Campbell centre fired a volley, and immediately the whole Royalist front responded and charged. We may well believe that the firing of famished men was wild, but it mattered little, for soon they were come, as Montrose wrote, "to push of pike and dint of sword." Alastair and O'Kean had little difficulty with the Lowland levies. In spite of the experience of many of them with Leven, a Highland charge was a new and awful thing to them, and they speedily broke and fled. Inverlochy was won by strategy, for of tactics there was little, and that little was elementary.

The gallant Campbell centre, indeed, made a determined stand. They knew that they could hope for no mercy from their ancestral foes, and they were not forgetful of the honourable traditions of their race. But in time they also broke. Some rushed into the loch and tried in vain to reach the galley of their chief, now fleeing to safety; some fled to the tower of Inverlochy. Most scattered along the shore, and on that blue February noon there was a fierce slaughter from the mouth of Nevis down to the mouth of Loch Leven. The Lowlanders were given quarter, but, in spite of all his efforts, Montrose could win no mercy for the luckless Campbells. The green Diarmaid tartan was a badge of death that day. On the Royalist side only four perished; on the Covenant side the slain outnumbered the whole of Montrose's army. At least

1,500 fell in the battle and pursuit, and among them were Auchinbreck himself and forty of the Campbell barons. Well might Keppoch's bard exult fiercely over the issue :—

> "Through the land of my fathers the Campbells have come,
> The flames of their foray enveloped my home;
> Broad Keppoch in ruin is left to deplore,
> And my country is waste from the hill to the shore—
> Be it so! by St. Mary, there's comfort in store.
>
> "Through the braes of Lochaber a desert he made,
> And Glen Roy may be lost to the plough and the spade;
> Though the bones of my kindred, unhonoured, unurned,
> Mark the desolate path where the Campbells have burned—
> Be it so! *From that foray they never returned.*"

So ended one of the sternest and swiftest marches in the history of war. Inverlochy was in one respect a decisive victory, for it destroyed the clan power of Argyll, and from its terrible toll the Campbells as a fighting force never recovered. Alastair's policy was justified, and the MacDonalds were amply avenged; the heather, as the phrase went, was above the gale at last.* To Montrose at the moment it seemed even more. He thought that with the galley of Lorn fell also the blue flag of the Covenant. He wrote straightway to the King :—

> "Give me leave, in all humility, to assure Your Majesty that, through God's blessing, I am in the fairest hopes of reducing this kingdom to Your Majesty's obedience. And, if the measures I have concerted with your other loyal subjects fail me not, which they hardly can, I doubt not before

* The heather is the MacDonald badge, and the gale, or bog myrtle, the Campbell.

the end of this summer I shall be able to come to Your Majesty's assistance with a brave army, which, backed with the justice of Your Majesty's cause, will make the rebels in England, as well as in Scotland, feel the just rewards of rebellion. Only give me leave, after I have reduced this country to Your Majesty's obedience, and conquered from Dan to Beersheba, to say to Your Majesty then, as David's general did to his master, 'Come thou thyself, lest this country be called by my name.' "

It was not to be. He was to win other astonishing victories, but before the year closed Philiphaugh was to be fought and the great adventure was to end in exile. Five years later, on a May day in the High Street of Edinburgh, there closed on the gallows the career of the bravest of Scottish hearts.

General Leslie.

VIII

THE FLIGHT OF LIEUTENANTS PARER AND M'INTOSH ACROSS THE WORLD

During the Great War there were thousands of hurried journeys made by airmen in the course of their military duties, and since November 1918 there have been many adventurous flights against time, in competition for this or that prize. But the story I propose to tell is, to my mind, wilder and more inconceivable than any episode in the history of aircraft in the War. It was not strictly a journey against time, for though the two airmen began by intending to compete in the Australian Flight competition, they were not able to leave Britain till Sir Ross Smith had reached Port Darwin. But the element of haste was not wanting, for all they possessed was a condemned comic-opera machine, which was rapidly going to pieces on their hands. Mr. Kipling has told the story of the tramp *Bolivar*, and of how that unseaworthy hulk was brought across the Bay in a state of impending dissolution. But if the *Bolivar* "bluffed the eternal sea," D.H.9 for seven months bluffed the powers of the air and flew, a derelict 'bus, 15,000 miles over land and water. It seems to me the craziest adventure that ever, by habitually taking the one chance in ten thousand, managed to succeed.

Lieutenant Raymond John Paul Parer was the son of a shopkeeper in Melbourne, a small, slight, dark man with a considerable turn for mechanics. During the War he was employed at training aerodromes in Britain, and was accustomed to fly new machines across to France. Lieutenant John Cowe M'Intosh was a large, raw-boned Scot from Banffshire, with a rugged masterful face, who had served through the War with the Australian forces. To begin with he knew nothing about air mechanics, and picked up the science as he went along. The two, being in England after the Armistice, made up their mind to fly back to Australia. They had no money, and it occurred to them that they might earn the £10,000 prize by entering for the Australia Flight competition. They received very little encouragement from the Air Ministry, for both men were wholly unpractised in long-distance flights, and had no previous knowledge of the route or of any language but their own. They managed, however, to raise from a friend a little money, and with this they purchased from the Disposals Board a single-engined two-seater D.H.9 bombing machine, their intention being to carry extra petrol in place of bombs. The engine was a Siddeley-Puma of 240 h.p. Complete ignorance in their case was the parent of courage. They were roughly aware of the possible stages by which they might take their route, and resolved to nose their way from one to another and trust to luck. It was like a man in an ill-found and leaky boat starting to cross the stormy Atlantic. Almost every part of their machine had some bad fault or other of which they were vaguely aware and expected further news.

They were not long in getting it. On January 8, 1920, they left Hounslow, intending to make the first landing at Paris. But a contrary wind and a thick fog forced them to land at Conteville, and when they reached Paris their petrol pump failed and compelled them to wait three days. After that they flew to Lyons, where the pump gave trouble again and delayed them another two days.

Then came the Gulf of Genoa. But they had hardly started when their oil ran out and they were compelled to return and fly 100 miles along the Italian coast without oil pressure, looking for a landing-place. Italy presented a series of mischances. The weather was abominable, and they crossed the Apennines at a height of 14,000 feet. There they were almost frozen, and for two and a half hours could see nothing of the ground. Later, at an altitude of 3,000 feet, their machine caught fire, and they were compelled to cut off the petrol and side-slip to land.

Brindisi was at length reached, and they had to face the crossing of the Adriatic. Somehow or other they reached Athens, where they had more engine trouble, and then staggered on to Crete. From Crete they flew the 220 miles of the Mediterranean to Mersa Matruh in Western Egypt, and eventually, on 21st February, reached Cairo.

The scheduled flying time from England to Cairo is under forty hours; but the trip had taken them forty-four days. They had now established the routine of their journey, which was to break down every day or two, and then patch up the machine with oddments sufficient to carry it to the next landing-place, where it fell to pieces again.

For four days at the Helouan aerodrome the two laboured at their crazy 'bus. Their propeller was defective; there were endless carburation troubles; the bolts—propeller, bearer, and cylinder—were always working loose; magnetos, oil filters, everything, were imperfect; the instruments were always failing, especially the air-speed indicator. And they had flown all the way to Egypt without cleaning their plugs!

On 26th February they set off again, making a beeline for Bagdad—a direct flight which no airman had ever before accomplished. For the enterprise, and still more for the continuation of the journey to Australia, they had no assets whatever, except a letter of authority from the General Officer Commanding R.A.F. Depots, which entitled them to draw for petrol on any depot along the route between Cairo and Delhi. It did not seem on the remote edge of possibility that much use would be made of that letter.

Nevertheless that day they crossed the desert of Sinai and landed safely at Ramleh. Thence they shaped their course across Arabia, an adventure in which, as we have seen, they were in the strictest sense pioneers. The weather changed to their disadvantage, and they drove on into head winds and heavy sheets of rain. A breakdown in the midst of the desert meant either starvation or robbery, and probably murder, by Arab tribes, and sure enough the breakdown came. They were compelled to make a forced landing in the evening, and had to spend the night on the ground by their machine. In the early morning they observed a crowd of Arabs approaching with obviously hostile intent. But the two airmen, having dared so much, were not to be awed by casual Bedouin. They happened to have some Mills bombs aboard, and with these and their revolvers they routed the enemy and kept him at bay until such time as they could start again.

Bagdad was reached eventually, entirely by luck and not at all by good guiding. There they were welcomed by the British air posts, and speeded on their way across Baluchistan and the Gulf of Kutch to Karachi, which they reached without mishap on 8th March. In India they fell in with Captain G. C. Matthews of the Australian Flying Corps, and in his Sopwith machine "Wallaby" he accompanied them across the peninsula to Delhi, where they had a busy time patching up D.H.9. The old relic was suffering

A crowd of Arabs approaching with obviously hostile intent.

See page 152.

from almost every ailment to which an aeroplane is subject. For one thing the central section was beginning to rise above the level of the wings, and they could only remedy the defect by packing with iron washers. The fabric, through constant exposure, was rotten, and the coats of ordinary motor-car paint with which it had been treated were peeling off in great patches. It was breaking away, too, all along the ribs, and they had to renew it there as best they could. Their first propeller had been damaged by taking off from the desert sands and had been renewed at Bagdad. Every assistance was given them by the R.A.F. officers in India, but it was not easy to patch up the unpatchable.

From Delhi they flew safely across the Bay of Bengal to Rangoon, but were compelled to make a forced landing in thick forest on the bank of the Irawaddy River, which did not improve the condition of D.H.9.

On 4th April they reached Rangoon and flew on another hundred miles to Moulmein. There, however, D.H.9 struck work. It crashed, and was so seriously damaged that they had to sit down quietly for no less than six weeks before they could resume their journey. Everything all at once seemed to dissolve into its parent elements. Their compasses were crocked; their radiator was in pieces; the under-carriage had at last collapsed completely, and the new propeller acquired at Bagdad was destroyed. Happily they managed to get a propeller of the Caproni type from a depot established there by the organizers of the Rome–Tokio flight. But the propeller had been designed for a 300 h.p. Fiat, and the result of fitting it to a 240 h.p. Siddeley-Puma meant a serious over-running of the engine. It was found, too, that the diameter of the Caproni "boss" was much larger than that of the D.H.9 shaft, so the gap was blocked with a Burmese wood which is so heavy that it will not float and so hard that it blunts the sharpest tool.

A new under-carriage was constructed out of a tough, close-grained native timber, which they bought from a local Chinaman. The wood was seasoned in an oven, and the new under-carriage was modelled from the assembled debris of the old one. They improvised a new radiator by taking a couple of ordinary "Overland" motor-car radiators and bolting them together!

Thus equipped, after six weeks' delay they started again, but presently they had another crash—a nose-dive in Batavia. This meant another delay, and a fourth propeller was got through the efforts of the British consul and the Dutch authorities. But before they left Dutch territory they had still another mishap, and a fifth propeller had to be found. Here the Dutch Air Force came to the rescue. They sent to their depot 400 miles away for spares, and provided a new under-carriage. Moreover, they lent the travellers two air mechanics, who worked under their supervision and managed to bring D.H.9 into some semblance of working order.

Meantime, through these weeks of sojourn in tropical lands, the machine had been converted into a sort of menagerie, and various strange animals made the fuselage their home, and only showed themselves in mid air. Among the beasts which thus added themselves to the party were bear cubs, a selection of lizards, several snakes, a whole congregation of rats and mice, and a baby alligator!

The next stage of the journey—the flight to Australia over 400 miles of sea—was the most anxious of all. It began unpromisingly, for D.H.9 had great difficulty in getting over the mountains of the island of Timor. When the ocean was reached the travellers discovered that they had lost their bearings; but the intrepid pair pushed on boldly into the unknown. For eight hours they journeyed in the void, and when their oil was almost run out they were at last greeted by the sight of land. On the last day of July, with one pint of petrol left, they landed at Fanny Bay in the Northern Territory. Next morning, the 1st of August, they reached Port Darwin.

They had achieved the journey to Australia, but their troubles were not over. They struggled on to Sydney, where, at the Mascot aerodrome on 22nd August, they were welcomed by an immense crowd of nearly 20,000 people. But Melbourne was their goal, and on the journey to Melbourne D.H.9 met its doom. At Culcairn it nose-dived into the earth at a speed of 70 miles an hour, and only the amazing luck of the travellers saved their necks. Another machine was provided for them, and on 31st August they finished their journey of 15,000 miles by reaching Flemington Racecourse at Melbourne. Accompanied by the battered remnants of D.H.9 they were officially welcomed by Mr. Hughes, the Commonwealth Prime Minister, to whom they presented a bottle of whisky, which they had brought with them intact from London. A day or two later they were formally received in Parliament Buildings and each presented with £500.

" The world is richer and better for what you have done," Mr. Hughes told them, and he spoke the truth. Their achievement was like the attempts to ascend Mount Everest—utterly useless in any prosaic sense, but a vindication of the vigour and daring of the human spirit. The history of aircraft is only beginning, but it is not likely that it will show any feat more wildly temerarious than that of these two amateurs, who drove a crazy machine through every type of weather and over every type of country from the snowy Apennines to the Malayan forests—always in difficulties, always resourceful and undaunted, till by sheer resolution they forced reluctant Fortune to yield to their importunity.

It seems to be the fate of great airmen, after daring the apparently impossible, to meet disaster in humdrum flights. Lieutenant M'Intosh was to go the way of Sir John Alcock and Sir Ross Smith, for on 29th March of the following year he was killed through his machine crashing in a small town in Western Australia.

IX

LORD NITHSDALE'S ESCAPE

THE first of the great Jacobite rebellions, that of 1715, was grossly mismanaged from the start. The invasion of England by the Scottish Catholic lords and the Northumbrian Jacobites came to a dismal close at Preston, and the Tower of London was soon full of exalted personages—the English Earl of Derwentwater, who was a grandson of Charles II., and the Scottish Earls of Wintoun, Nithsdale, and Carnwath, and Lord Kenmure, who was head of the Galloway Gordons. The trial of the Jacobite lords was not a masterpiece of English justice. The method followed was impeachment, and it was clear from the start that, with a Protestant House of Commons, Catholic rebels had no kind of chance. Without proper proof they were condemned—a political, rather than a legal verdict. They were advised to plead guilty, which as it turned out was an unwise course, for thereby they trusted their lives to the Crown and not to the English law, and King George's Government were determined to make an example of them as a matter of policy. Wintoun alone refused to plead.

But the people of England were more merciful than their Government, and the popular feeling in favour of leniency was so strong that Walpole was unable to send all the lords to the scaffold. For Derwentwater there could be no mercy; he was too near in blood to the royal house. Nithsdale and Kenmure were also marked for death, partly because they were devouter Catholics than the others, and partly because of their great power in the Lowlands. On Thursday, February 23, 1716, the Lord Chancellor signed the warrants for their execution on the Saturday.

Derwentwater and Kenmure duly lost their heads, and two famous houses were brought to ruin. But when the guards arrived to summon Nithsdale to the scaffold they found that he was gone. This is the story of his escape.

The Countess of Nithsdale had been Lady Winifred Herbert, the youngest daughter of the first Marquis of Powis. At the time she was twenty-six years of age, a slim young woman with reddish hair and pale blue eyes. Her family had always been Catholic and Royalist, and she had shown herself one of the most ardent of Jacobite ladies.

When the news came of the rout at Preston she was at Terregles, the home of the Maxwells in Nithsdale. She realized at once that her husband could expect no mercy, and that his death must follow his imprisonment as certainly as night follows day. It was a bitter January, with snowdrifts on every road. Without wasting an hour she set off for the south after burning incriminating papers. Her only attendant was a Welsh girl called Evans, from the Powis estates, who had been her maid since childhood.

The two women and a groom rode through the wintry country to Newcastle, where they took the coach for York. Presently the coach stuck in the snow, and word came that all the roads were blocked. But by offering a large sum Lady Nithsdale managed to hire horses, and pushed on into the Midlands. The little company suffered every kind of disaster, but the lady's resolute spirit overcame them all, and after some days of weary travel they reached London.

Lady Nithsdale went straight to some of the Scottish great ladies, such as the Duchess of Buccleuch and the Duchess of Montrose, and heard from them that the worst might be expected. She realized that no appeal could save the prisoner, and that, unless he could break bar and bolt, in a week she would be a widow. The first step was to get admission to the Tower. Walpole refused to let her see her husband unless she was prepared to share his captivity to the end. She declined the condition, for she understood that if she was to do anything she must be free. At last she succeeded in bribing the keepers, and found herself in her husband's chamber. As she looked round she saw that there was no chance of an ordinary escape. One high barred window gave on the ramparts and Water Lane, and a sentry was on guard in front. If Lord Nithsdale were to leave the Tower he must leave it by the door. That in turn was strongly guarded. A halberdier stood outside and two sentries with fixed bayonets, and the stairs and the outer door were equally well held. Force was out of the question. The only hope lay in ingenuity.

The weak part of any prison is to be found in the human warders, more especially in a place so strong as the Tower, where the ordinary avenues of escape are few and difficult. The Lieutenant, trusting in his walls, was inclined to be negligent. The prison rules were often disregarded, and the wives and children of the officials wandered about the passages at will. This gave Lady Nithsdale her plan. She proposed to her husband to dress him up in cap and skirt and false curls and pass him as a woman through the soldiers. Very soon she had worked out the details. She had women friends who would assist: a Miss Hilton, and the landlady, Mrs. Mills, at her lodging in Drury Lane. The latter was tall and inclined to be stout, and a riding-hood that fitted her would fit Lord Nithsdale, while a red wig would counterfeit

Mrs. Mill's hair. The prisoner's black eyebrows could be painted out, his chin shaved and his skin rouged.

Lord Nithsdale stubbornly refused. The scheme seemed to him crazy. How could a stalwart soldier with a rugged face and a martial stride imitate any woman? He might do something with a sword in his hand, but, raddled and painted, he would only be a laughing-stock. Far better let his wife get a petition from him placed in the royal hands. There might be some hope in that.

Lady Nithsdale pretended to agree, though she knew well that the King's clemency was a broken reed. For George had given strict orders that no petition from Lord Nithsdale should be received, and she found her friends very unwilling to disobey the King and act as intermediaries. Her only hope was to see George himself; so she dressed herself in deep black, and, accompanied by Miss Hilton, who knew the King by sight, went to Court. They reached the room between the King's apartment and the main drawing-room, and when George appeared she flung herself before him. "I am the wretched Countess of Nithsdale," she cried. The King stepped back, refusing to take the petition; but she caught him by the skirt of his coat and poured out her story in French. George lost his temper, but she would not let go, and suffered herself to be dragged along the floor to the drawing-room door. There the officials unclasped her fingers and released his angry Majesty.

Lord Nithsdale now turned his hopes to the House of Lords. The Countess went from peer to peer; but once again she failed. Lord Pembroke, indeed, who was a kinsman, spoke in favour of the prisoner, but the thing was hopeless from the start. Nithsdale was utterly intractable and impenitent, and would never beg for his life.

Her husband's counsels having failed, it remained to follow her own. She drove to the Tower and told all the guards and keepers that Lord Nithsdale's last petition to the House of Lords had been favourably received, and that His Majesty was about to listen to their prayer. The officials congratulated her, for she had made herself very popular amongst them, and their friendliness was increased by her gifts. But to her husband she told the plain truth. The last moment had come. Next day was Friday, when the King would answer the petition. If he refused, as he was certain to do, on Saturday the prisoner would go to the scaffold.

On that Friday morning she completed her plans with Mrs. Mills, and as the January dusk drew in Miss Hilton joined them in Drury Lane and the details were finally settled. Miss Hilton was to be a friend, "Mrs. Catherine," and Mrs. Mills another friend, "Mrs. Betty." With the maid Evans all three would drive to the Tower, where Evans would wait inconspicuously near the Lieutenant's door, and the other three women would go to the earl's chamber. Miss Hilton, being slim, was to wear two riding-hoods, her own and that of Mrs. Mills. When she was in the room she was to drop her extra clothes and leave at once. Mrs. Mills was then to go in as "Mrs. Betty," wearing a riding-hood to fit the earl. She was to be weeping bitterly and holding a handkerchief to her face. Everything depended upon Miss Hilton being able to slip away quietly; then Mrs. Mills, having diminished in size, was to depart as "Mrs. Catherine," while the earl was to go out as "Mrs. Betty." The vital point was to get the sentries thoroughly confused as to who had gone in and out.

They drove in a coach to the Tower, and Lady Nithsdale, in order to keep the others from doleful anticipations, chattered the whole way. When they reached the Tower they found several women in the Council Chamber who had come to see Lady Nithsdale pass, for they had a suspicion, in spite of her cheerfulness, that this was the last occasion on which she would see her husband alive. The presence of these women, who were all talking together, helped to confuse the sentries. Lady Nithsdale took in Miss Hilton first, naming her "Mrs. Catherine." Miss Hilton at once shed her extra clothing and then left, Lady Nithsdale accompanying her to the staircase and crying, "Send my maid to me at once. I must be dressed without delay or I shall be too late for my petition." Then Mrs. Mills came up the stairs, a large fat woman sobbing bitterly and apparently all confused with grief. She was greeted by the Countess as "Mrs. Betty," and taken into Lord Nithsdale's room. There she changed her clothes, dried her tears, and went out with her head up and a light foot. "Good-bye, my dear Mrs. Catherine," Lady Nithsdale cried after her. "Don't omit to send my maid. She cannot know how late it is. She has forgotten that I am to present the petition to-night." The women in the Council Chamber watched Mrs. Mills's departure with sympathy, and the sentry opened the door for her to pass.

Now came the great moment. If any single keeper in the outer room had kept his wits about him the plot must be discovered. Everything depended upon their being confused among the women, and believing that "Mrs. Betty" was still with the Countess in Lord Nithsdale's chamber. It was nearly dark and in a few minutes lights would be brought in, and a single candle would betray them. The Countess took off all her petticoats save one and tied them round her husband. There was no time to shave him, so she wrapped a muffler round his chin. His cheeks were rouged; false ringlets were tied around his brow; and a great riding-hood was put on. Then the Countess opened the door and led him by the hand. Her voice was now sharp with anxiety. "For the love of God," she cried, "my dear Mrs. Betty, run and bring her with you.

The sentries in the dim light were unsuspicious and let them pass.

See page 166.

You know my lodgings, and if ever you hurried in your life, hurry now. I am driven mad with this delay."

The sentries in the dim light were unsuspicious and let them pass; indeed, one of them opened the chamber door. The Countess slipped behind her husband in the passage, so that no one looking after him should see his walk, which was unlike that of any woman ever born. "Make haste, make haste," she cried, and then, almost before she had realized it, they had passed the last door and the sentries.

Evans, the maid, was waiting, and seizing Lord Nithsdale, *alias* "Mrs. Betty," by the arm, hurried him off to a house near Drury Lane. There he was dressed in the livery of a servant of the Venetian Minister, and started for the coast.

The Countess, dreading lest some keeper should enter her husband's room and find him gone, rushed back there with a great appearance of distress and slammed the door. Then for a few minutes she strolled about with the step of a heavy man, and carried on an imaginary conversation, imitating his gruff replies. Now came the last stage. She raised the latch, and, standing in the doorway so that all the crowd in the Council Chamber could hear, bade her husband good-night with every phrase of affection. She declared that something extraordinary must have happened to Evans, and that there was nothing for it but to go herself and see. She added that if the Tower were open she would come back that night. Anyhow, she hoped to be with him early in the morning, bringing him good news. As she spoke she drew the latch-string through the hole and banged the door. "I pray you, do not disturb my lord," she said in passing. "Do not send him candles till he calls for them. He is now at his prayers." The unsuspicious sentries saluted her with sympathy. Beyond the outer gate was a waiting coach in which she drove at once to tell the

Duchess of Montrose what had been done. Meantime Lord Nithsdale, dressed as an Italian servant, was posting along the road to Dover, where, next morning, he found a boat for Calais. It was not long before his wife rejoined him in Rome.

Lady Nithsdale's bold escapade was received by the people of England with very general approval. Even the Government, who were beginning to have doubts about the wisdom of their policy, were not disposed to be too severe on the heroic wife. When the Duchess of Montrose went to Court next day she found the King very angry. But the royal anger was short-lived. Presently he began to laugh. "Upon my soul," he said, "for a man in my lord's situation it was the very best thing he could have done."

Earl of Mar.
(*Jacobite leader.*)

Queen Elizabeth.

X

SIR ROBERT CARY'S RIDE TO EDINBURGH

THE history of these islands is strewn with tales of swift and fateful rides, but as a rule the distances were short. In old days it was nobody's business to get in a hurry from Land's End to John o' Groats, and long journeys, even the marches of the Edwards into Scotland, were leisurely affairs. But though roads were infamous, horses were as good then as now, and if a man were called upon for an extended journey against time he could make a record on horseback that was scarcely surpassed till the days of steam. Queen Mary, after the Battle of Langside, rode the 92 miles through the western moorlands to the shores of the Solway without, as she said, drawing rein, though I presume there were changes of mount. That, indeed, is the essence of the business, for no horse ever foaled can keep its pace beyond a certain limit. The present writer once, in his youth, rode 75 miles in the Northern Transvaal at a stretch on one horse; but, after the Boer fashion, he off-saddled every two hours for twenty minutes—a thing impossible in a really hustled journey.

This story tells of the ride of Sir Robert Cary from London to Edinburgh with the news of the death of Elizabeth. The distance by any road was little less than 400 miles, but he probably took short cuts after he crossed the Border. He did the course in something under sixty hours—a most remarkable achievement. When William III. died at 8 a.m. on March 8, 1702, the news, though sent off at once, did not reach Edinburgh till 10 p.m. on 11th March—85 hours. Cary's record was not indeed approached till the days of post-chaises and flying mails. In 1832 the Reform Bill passed the Lords at 6.35 a.m. on Saturday, 14th April. Sixty-five minutes later Mr. Young of *The Sun* newspaper left the Strand in a post-chaise and four, with copies of the paper containing a report of the debate and the division, and on Sunday, at 7.30 p.m., he arrived at the house of his agent in Glasgow. The distance was 403 miles, and it was covered in 35 hours 50 minutes.*

Five years later, when the completion of Telford's new Carlisle–Glasgow road had reduced the distance to 397 miles, the mail which brought to Glasgow news of the death of William IV. left the General Post Office at 8 p.m. on 20th June and reached Glasgow at 2 p.m. on 22nd June—a total of 42 hours. But till 1832 Cary's record would seem to have held the field.

Now for the story. Sir Robert Cary, who afterwards became Earl of Monmouth, was the youngest of the ten sons of Henry Lord Hunsdon, who was a cousin of Queen Elizabeth. He had a varied and adventurous youth. As a very young man he visited Scotland with Walsingham, and thus formed his first acquaintance with King James. The Scottish king would have taken him into his service; but there were difficulties with Elizabeth, and young Cary consequently went to the Low Countries with the Earl of Essex. When Mary of Scots was beheaded he was chosen to carry Elizabeth's explanations to James in Scotland, and the following year he was again at Dumfries with the Scottish king, who was busy

* Mitchell's *Old Glasgow Essays*, pp. 195–196.

suppressing refractory Maxwells. In 1589, being very hard up, he wagered £2,000 with another courtier that he would walk the 300 miles to Berwick in twelve days. He won his bet, and thereafter, he tells us, was enabled to live for some time at Court like a gentleman. He must have been no mean pedestrian, and that in an age when the gentry rode too habitually to walk well.

After that he crossed the Channel again with Essex, and commanded a regiment with some distinction, so that he was knighted on the field by his general. When the French war was ended he found himself without employment and considerably in debt. He was lucky enough, however, to be appointed successor to old Lord Scroop, the Warden of the West Marches. The Scottish border was at that time divided into three Wardenships—the East Marches, from the sea to the Great Cheviot; the Middle Marches, from Cheviot to the Liddel; and the West Marches, extending to the Solway shore.

He was now in his early thirties, and for some years he led a stirring life, keeping order among the Armstrongs, Elliots, and Grahams in the "Debateable Land." Sir Robert was not the most elevated of characters; he was a true courtier, steering the frail barque of his fortunes with caution and skill in the difficult waters of the queen's favour. Once he was sent on a very confidential mission to James at Edinburgh, and seeing that the King of Scots must sooner or later come to the English throne, he laboured to stand well with him. Presently he became Deputy-Warden for his father in the East Marches, and was given the Captainship of Norham Castle on Tweed. There he had perpetual troubles with Sir Robert Ker of Cessford, the ancestor of the Dukes of Roxburghe, and on the whole got the better of that stalwart Borderer. There seems to have been little ill-will in the Marches in those days. Both sides laboured to outwit the other, but they bore no grudge for failure, and one month would be harrying each other's lands and the next hobnobbing at huntings and festivals. By and by Sir Robert Ker became his hostage and guest, and the two grew fast friends.

When Lord Hunsdon died Sir Robert was made Warden in his father's place, and with the help of the Fosters, Ridleys, Musgraves, Fenwicks, and Widdringtons, exercised a strong, if cautious, rule throughout the bounds of Cheviot. He led an expedition against the Armstrongs, who sheltered themselves in the Bog of Tarras, and by a swift march got in on their rear and made a large haul of prisoners. Sir Walter Scott, in his early journeyings in Liddesdale, found that the people there had still a tradition of what they called "Cary's raid." It was the most creditable period of his life, and he seems to have enjoyed it, for there was that in the man which delighted in alarums and excursions.

But once a courtier always a courtier. Throughout these stirring years Cary was perpetually haunted by anxiety as to how he stood in the Queen's favour, and when he could spare the time would go South to show himself at Court. At the end of the year 1602 he was in London and found Elizabeth very ill. "She took me by the hand and wrung it hard, and said, 'Young Robin, I am not well,' and then discoursed with me of her indisposition and that her heart had been sad and heavy for ten or twelve days; and in her discourse she fetched not so few as forty or fifty great sighs. I was grieved at first to see her in this plight, for of all my life before I never knew her fetch a sigh but when the Queen of Scots was beheaded."

The great Queen was now seventy years of age. All spring and summer she had been very well and had gone maying in the Lewisham woods. The Ambassador of Scotland had been kept waiting in corridors, as if to announce to his master that the time was far distant when he could transfer himself to Whitehall. In the autumn the Court had been especially gay; but Lord Worcester had noted that the Queen was failing, and that in the winter "the tune of Lullaby" would be the one wanted. In the middle of January 1603, on the insistence of her doctors, she moved to Richmond, where the Court and Council followed her. At first nothing would persuade her to go to bed; and when Nottingham and Cecil insisted she replied that the word "must" was not used to princes. "Little man, little man," she cried to Cecil, "if your father had lived you durst not have said so much; but you know I must die and that makes you presumptuous."

On the 22nd of March she was obviously sinking. She told Nottingham that only a king must succeed her, and when pressed to be more explicit, added, "Who should that be but our cousin of Scotland?" On Wednesday, 23rd March, she was speechless, and that afternoon called her Council to her bedchamber. When she was asked about her successor she put her hand to her head at the mention of the King of Scots, which the watchers interpreted to signify acquiescence. The archbishop and her chaplains remained with her praying during the night, and at about three on the morning of the 24th she died.

Cary was in a fever of impatience. He remembered his old acquaintance with King James, and realized that whoever took him the first news of the Queen's death would stand a good chance of rising high in his favour. But he was also aware that the Lords of the Council would do their best to prevent any unauthorized messenger, and that they certainly would not authorize him. On the night of the 23rd he went back to his lodging, leaving word with the servants of the Queen's household to let him know if it were likely the Queen would die, and giving the porter an angel to let him in at any time he called. Between one and two on Thursday morning he received a message that the Queen was at the point of death, and he hastened to the royal apartments. There at first he was forbidden entrance, the Lords of the Council having ordered that none should go in or out except by their warrant. But a friend managed to get him in, and passing through the waiting ladies in the ante-chamber he entered the privy chamber, where the Council was assembled. The Lords dealt with him brusquely, for they had divined his intention and forbade him to go to Scotland till they sent him. He then went to his brother's room, roused him, and made him accompany him to the gate. The porter could not refuse, in spite of the Council's orders, to let out Lord Hunsdon, and the zealous Sir Robert managed to follow in his train.

Cary was a man of action and did not let the grass grow under his feet. He rode straight to the Knight Marshal's lodging by Charing Cross, where he slept till morning. At nine o'clock he heard that the Lords of the Council were in the old orchard at Whitehall, and he sent the Marshal to tell them that he awaited their commands. They were determined that Cary should not move; but they told the Marshal to send for him, as if they meant to dispatch him at once to King James. One of them, however, Lord Banbury, whispered in the Marshal's ear that if Cary came he would be detained and another sent in his stead. The Marshal met Cary arriving at the gate, and told him the facts. Cary's mind was made up. He turned, mounted his horse, and rode for the North.

The start was made between nine and ten o'clock. The route was probably the Great North Road to Doncaster, where he slept the night, having covered 155 miles since the morning. Next day he reached his own house at Widdrington in Northumberland, the house of the March Warden, having left some very weary cattle on the road behind him. There he gave his deputies instructions to see to the peace of the Borders, and next morning to proclaim James King of

England at Morpeth and Alnwick. At dawn on Saturday, the 26th, he took the road again and reached his Castle of Norham about noon, travelling probably by the eastern end of the Cheviots and the town of Wooler.

It was a disastrous morning, for he had a bad fall and was kicked by his horse on the head, so that he lost much blood. But Cary was a true moss-trooper, and though forty-three years of age was as tough in body as any young Armstrong or Elliot. He did not tarry at Norham, but set off at once for Edinburgh, probably by the valley of the Leader and Soutra Hill. He complains that he was compelled to ride a " soft pace " because of his wounds, or he would have been in Edinburgh early in the evening in time for supper.

He finally arrived at Holyrood about nine or ten, and found that the King had gone to bed. Crying that he had great news for the royal ear, he was at once taken to the King's chamber, where he knelt and saluted James as Monarch of England, Scotland, Ireland, and France. The King gave him his hand to kiss and welcomed him kindly, listening eagerly to the tale of the Queen's sickness and death. He asked if there were any letters from the Council. But Cary explained the position and how narrowly he had escaped from them. But he gave the King "a blue ring from a fair lady " (I presume Queen Elizabeth), on which His Majesty said, " It is enough. I know by this you are a true messenger." Cary was handed over to Lord Home, with strict instructions for his entertainment, and the King's own surgeons were sent to look after him. When he kissed hands on departure, James thus addressed him : " I know you have lost a near kinswoman and a loving mistress ; but take here my hand. I will be as good a master to you, and will requite this service with honour and reward."

Sir Robert went to bed a happy man, and for a day or two his fortunes looked roseate. But presently came the bitter complaint by the Lords of the Council of his unauthorized performance, and he realized that James's gratitude was a brittle thing, and that he had too many competitors for the royal favour. For a year or two the poor moss-trooper was under a cloud. But his tough and wary spirit could not be permanently eclipsed, and before long he had risen again to favour. He accompanied Prince Charles and the Duke of Buckingham on their wild visit to Spain, and was given an earldom by King Charles I.

As I have said, his was no very elevated character, and his name lives in English history only because of his mad three days' ride, which for more than two hundred years was not equalled.

James VI. and I.

XI

THE ESCAPE OF PRINCESS CLEMENTINA

In the year 1718 the Chevalier de St. George, or, as some called him, the Old Pretender, after the defeat of his hopes in Scotland, had retired to Rome. At the age of thirty he was still a bachelor, but the unhappiness of his condition was due not to his celibacy but to his misfortunes. The Jacobite campaign of 1715 had proved a disastrous failure; and although he still retained the courtesy title of James III., he was a king without a realm. While the royal exile was twiddling his thumbs in the Italian capital, waiting for a better turn of luck, his friends, seeing that nothing further was to be gained by the pursuit of Mars, sought the aid of Cupid. They laid before the Chevalier the flattering proposal of a marriage with a Princess of beauty and race. This move was inspired less by romance than by politics, for a suitable marriage would not only encourage the waning Jacobite hopes, but might raise up an heir to the Cause.

The Chevalier readily concurred in the scheme, and a certain Mr. Charles Wogan was dispatched to the various European courts to report on a suitable bride for the Chevalier. Wogan's choice fell on the little Polish Princess Clementina Sobiesky, daughter of James Sobiesky of Poland and Edwige Elizabeth

Amelia of the house of Newburgh, and grand-daughter of the famous John Sobiesky, the "deliverer of Christendom."

The chronicles of the time are loud in the praises of this lady, her illustrious birth, her qualities of heart and mind, "her Goodness, Sweetness of Temper, and other Beauties of a valuable character." She is said to have been "happy in all the Charms, both of Mind and Body, her Sex can boast of"; "the Agreeableness of Seventeen and the Solidity of Thirty." Her accomplishments included Polish, High Dutch, French, Italian, and English, all of which she spoke so well that it was difficult to distinguish which of these languages was the most familiar to her. She was also a young woman of exemplary piety, and therefore a suitable bride for a king in exile. Princess Clementina was only sixteen when the Chevalier and his friends laid siege to her affections.

It was no ordinary business, for there were many hazards and difficulties in the way. The Chevalier had given his consent to the proposed alliance; it was for his friends to see it brought to a successful issue, and the plan of campaign was left entirely in their hands. The bridegroom was a mere pawn—a willing pawn—in the game. The real difficulty was the House of Hanover, the inveterate enemy of the Stuart cause, which was by no means inclined to look with indulgence on the proposed alliance. Although the affair was kept a profound secret, the matter gradually leaked out; and George I. of England protested with such vigour to the Emperor on the folly and danger of the impending marriage, threatening among other things to break up the Quadruple Alliance, that Princess Clementina was arrested at Innsbrück with her mother and kept there under strict surveillance.

The Chevalier and his friends were in a quandary. Obviously a man built in the heroic mould was necessary to extricate them from the dilemma. They bethought them of Wogan, who had been recalled from his delicate mission on the pretext that it was impolitic to entrust the matter further to an Irish Catholic. Wogan was well adapted for this sort of adventure. He was, besides being something of a poet, a cavalier and a courtier. He had shared the hard fortunes of the Chevalier in Scotland, and had suffered imprisonment for his devotion to the Stuart cause. Once more the soldier of fortune was called upon to prove his devotion in a cause no less hazardous.

The Pope, who had been taken into the secret, had provided Wogan with a passport in the name of the Comte de Cernes, and forth he fared like a fairy-tale knight to rescue a distressed princess. Never had d'Artagnan and his Musketeers a more difficult task. Wogan duly arrived at Innsbrück in the disguise of a merchant, and obtained an interview with the Princess and her mother, who heartily concurred in the proposed plan of a secret "elopement." We next find him at Ohlau in quest of the Prince Sobiesky, the lady's father. Here he met with a rebuff. Prince Sobiesky, a practical man of the world, viewed the whole affair as midsummer madness, and absolutely refused to lend his aid or consent to Wogan's scheme.

Wogan was in a quandary, but he did not lose heart. He had nothing to complain of during his stay with Prince Sobiesky, for he was well lodged and treated with the most flattering attentions, but the real business of the mission hung fire. Still he waited—he had long learned the game of patience — and, being a courtier, was used to waiting. At length a happy accident turned the scale in his favour. On New Year's Day, Prince Sobiesky, as a mark of his esteem, presented his guest with a magnificent snuff-box, formed of a single turquoise set in gold, a family heirloom, and part of the treasure found by John Sobiesky in the famous scarlet pavilion of Kara Mustapha. Wogan, with a charming gesture, declined the gift on the plea that, although he was sensible of the high honour shown him by the Prince, he could not think of returning to Italy with a present for himself and a refusal for his master. The Prince was so touched that he finally yielded, and furnished Wogan with the necessary instructions to his wife and daughter. Wogan set out once more on his adventures in high spirits, carrying not only the precious instructions, but the snuff-box, which Prince Sobiesky had pressed on him as a parting gift.

The next thing was to establish secret communication with the Princess. This was more easily said than done. The garrulity of Prince Sobiesky, who in his parental agitation had babbled the whole story to a certain German baron, and the suspicions of the Countess de Berg, a noted *intriguante* and spy of the Austrian court, almost brought Wogan's mission to an inglorious end. The baron was bought over at "considerable expenditure," but the Countess was a more difficult matter. While Wogan was the guest of honour of Prince Sobiesky she had been puzzled at the attentions shown to him, which she argued could be for no good end, and set her spies on his track. Wogan escaped by the skin of his teeth, and only evaded capture by ostentatiously announcing his departure for Prague. Then by a skilful detour he gave his pursuers the slip and posted on to Vienna, where he vainly tried to enlist the sympathy of the Papal Nuncio, Monseigneur Spinola.

Then came a thunderbolt, for suddenly Prince Sobiesky changed his mind. He dispatched an urgent message to Wogan, saying that both the Princess and her mother, alarmed at the dangers that encompassed them, had resolved to proceed no further in the business, and that he forthwith cancelled his previous instructions.

Here was a pretty kettle of fish! Wogan was a stout-hearted fellow, but this new blow almost unmanned him. In his dilemma he wrote to the Chevalier and told the whole story, asking him at the same time to send a confidential servant to obtain fresh powers from Prince Sobiesky. The Chevalier promptly dispatched one of his valets, a Florentine called Michael Vezzosi, who, when attached to a Venetian Embassy in London, had been instrumental in aiding the escape of Lord Nithsdale from the Tower. The Chevalier reminded Prince Sobiesky that by his foolish behaviour he was not only needlessly endangering the lives of Wogan and his friends, but adding to the difficulties of the captives at Innsbrück. He also gave the most explicit instructions to Wogan to proceed with the enterprise.

Wogan accordingly set out for Schlettstadt, where he met his three kinsmen, Major Gaydon and Captains Misset and O'Toole, who were to lend their aid in the now difficult mission. Mrs. Misset accompanied her husband, together with her maid Jeanneton, but neither of the women was told the real nature of the undertaking. Jeanneton was to play a conspicuous part in the escape of Clementina. Wogan's plan was that the maid should change places with the Princess, and generally impersonate her till she had made good her escape. The light-headed girl was told a cock-and-bull story about O'Toole having fallen violently in love with a beautiful heiress, and Wogan played to such a tune on her sense of the romantic that she gleefully entered into the plot of the "elopement."

Wogan, however, was not yet out of the wood. So far he had succeeded, but he had now to deal with the whims and caprice of the ladies who had been pressed into the enterprise. Jeanneton, whose importance to the success of the venture was paramount, proved especially troublesome. First of all she refused point-blank to wear the low-heeled shoes which had been specially ordered for her, so as to reduce her height to conformity with that of the Princess; and not only screamed and swore, but went so far in her tantrums as to knock the shoemaker down. She had once been a camp-follower, and her manners were those of the tented field. It was not until Mrs. Misset, in an excess of despair, had thrown herself imploringly at her feet, a ceremony in which the gentlemen of the party were constrained to join, that the maid relented, and the party set forth at last in a ramshackle berline for Innsbrück.

So far so good. At an inn between Nassereith and Innsbrück, while the other members of the party regaled themselves with a banquet of wild boar and sauerkraut, Wogan stole out in the rain to keep an important appointment with a certain M. Châteaudoux, gentleman-usher to the Princess Sobiesky. This gentleman had not Wogan's spirit, and proposed to defer the matter of the escape till the weather had cleared and the roads were in better condition for travel. Wogan firmly waved aside his objections, and succeeded so well in convincing him that now or never was the time, that at half-past eleven that same night he and the precious Jeanneton made their way in the storm to the *schloss* where the Princess was confined. Fortune smiled on the enterprise, and even the tempest was propitious, for the sentry, heedless of danger on such a night, had sought refuge in the inn.

Meanwhile within the prison walls the Princess Clementina, in order to assist the plan of escape, was playing the part of an invalid. Jeanneton's rôle was simple. The Princess having regained her freedom, all that the maid had to do was to keep her bed on the plea that her megrims were no better, refusing to see any one but her mother. The secret was well kept; not even the governess was told, lest her grief at the sudden departure of the Princess might arouse suspicions.

At midnight, according to plan, Châteaudoux was in readiness, and Jeanneton, clad in a shabby riding hood

She followed Châteaudoux down the winding stairs and out into the night.

See page 184.

and female surtout, was successfully smuggled into the sleeping chamber of the Princess. Wogan and O'Toole waited at the street corner ready to convoy the Princess to the inn. There was a lengthy farewell scene between the Princess and her mother. The two having wept and embraced each other, Clementina excused herself for her hurried departure on the plea that nothing in heaven or earth must stand in the way between her and her husband. Then she hastily dressed herself in Jeanneton's clothes, and followed Châteaudoux down the winding stairs and out into the night.

The Princess was no longer a captive. The tempest, which had increased, favoured the escape. Once more successfully evading the sentry, they quickly gained the street corner where Wogan and O'Toole were kicking their heels, consumed with fear and anxiety. They reached the inn, drenched to the skin, with but one slight misadventure. Clementina, mistaking a floating wisp of hay for a solid log of wood, slipped and plunged over the ankles into a channel of half-melted snow. At the inn she eagerly swallowed a cup of hot spiced wine and changed her soaking garments. Konski, her mother's page, had followed meanwhile with what the chronicles of the period call " inside apparel " and a casket containing her jewels, said to be valued at about 150,000 pistoles. The foolish Konski, no doubt scared out of his wits at his share in the adventure, had thrown the precious packet behind the door and taken ignominiously to his heels.

They were now ready for the road. Captain Misset, who had gone out to reconnoitre, having returned with a favourable report, off they started. The inn was silent and shuttered, everybody having retired for the night including the landlady ; so they stole off unobserved. As the ancient coach lumbered past the dismal *schloss* where the Princess had been so recently a prisoner, she could not restrain some natural emotion at the thought of her mother ; and then suddenly she discovered the loss of the precious packet. Here was a nice to-do! There was nothing for it but to return to the inn and fetch the packet. O'Toole was entrusted with this anxious mission. By one more stroke of good fortune he succeeded in retrieving it from behind the door where the careless Konski had thrown it, but he had first to prise the door off its crazy hinges.

At sunset the party reached the village of Brenner, where the Princess, who had so far borne up nobly, had a slight attack of the vapours. She was speedily revived, however, by a dose of eau de Carmes, and, having had a meal, soon regained her accustomed gaiety, and began to ply Wogan with all sorts of innocent questions about the manners and customs of the English and his adventures with the Chevalier in Scotland. One by one the party dropped off to sleep, all but Wogan, who as the Master of the Ceremonies, managed to keep himself awake by the expedient of taking prodigious pinches of snuff. At last even he, overcome by the ardours of the night, began to show signs of drowsiness. While dropping off to sleep, his snuff-box accidentally slipped from his lap and fell on to the curls of the Princess, who with her head resting against his knees was reposing at the bottom of the carriage.

Verona was still a journey of forty-six hours, and the party were much inconvenienced by the lack of post-horses. To their horror they discovered that they were travelling in the wake of the Princess of Baden and her son, one of the husbands who had been proposed for Clementina, and whom she had been actually bribed to marry! At another stage of the journey the coachman was drunk, and they were only saved by a miracle from being dashed to pieces at the foot of one of the precipitous gorges of the Adige.

They were now approaching the most difficult part of the journey, and it was arranged before they passed the frontier of the Venetian States that O'Toole and Misset should remain behind to intercept any messengers from Innsbrück and guard the retreat. This prescience was amply rewarded. O'Toole had soon the satisfaction of waylaying a courier who had been dispatched in hot pursuit of the fugitive. The fellow was not only put entirely off the scent, but at supper was plied so generously with old brandy that he had to be carried drunk to bed. Having relieved him of his documents the cavaliers rode on to rejoin the party in the berline.

One or two trials had still to be overcome. At Trent there was some delay owing to the behaviour of a surly Governor who put every obstacle in their way. There was besides the continual fear of Clementina being detected by her Highness of Baden, who had installed herself in state at the inn. The poor little Princess had perforce to remain hidden at the bottom of the coach in the public square until such time as they could obtain fresh relays. The best they could find was a couple of tired screws taken from a neighbouring field. At Roveredo things were even worse, as no horses were to be had at all; and to crown their misfortunes they had not proceeded six miles with their weary beasts when the axle of the ramshackle old berline broke!

But at length they reached the great white wall that denoted the boundary between the Venetian States and the dominions of the Emperor. At half-past three in the morning they stole across the frontier and solemnly offered up a *Te Deum* for their safe deliverance. They reached Pery with the bells merrily ringing for Mass, and narrowly missed being recognized by the Princess of Baden, who with her son was just entering the church when the berline drew up at the church door.

Verona was reached at dusk, and here for the first time during the three days' journey the Princess had her hair dressed. They came to Bologna on 2nd May, where the Princess sent a message to the Cardinal Origo announcing her arrival. The Cardinal speedily repaired to pay his respects, bringing the present of a "toyley, artificial flowers, and other little things," and the offer of a box at the Opera. More welcome and important than the courtesies of the Cardinal was the arrival of Mr. Murray, the Chevalier's agent, with messages from his royal master.

The drama of the royal elopement draws to its close. On 9th May Clementina was married by proxy. The little Princess, all agog with excitement, rose at 5 a.m., and having attired herself in a white dress and a pearl necklace went to Mass and received the Holy Communion. The marriage ceremony was performed by an English priest. The Chevalier was represented by Mr. Murray, with Wogan as witness, and Prince Sobiesky by the Marquis of Monte-Boularois, a loyal friend of the Stuart cause. The "powers" of the Chevalier were read publicly on conclusion of the Mass, setting forth his willingness to marry the Princess Clementina Sobiesky, and the ceremony was forthwith performed with the ring which he had sent expressly for the purpose.

The Princess entered Rome on 15th May, amid general rejoicings; and on 2nd September a public marriage was celebrated at Montefiascone.

The daring flight and escape of the Princess Clementina caused some sensation at the time, and a medal was struck to commemorate the event. The Chevalier created Wogan a baronet, as well as his three kinsmen, and Wogan had the further distinction of being made a Roman Senator by Pope Clement XI. Jeanneton, who had played her part well, apart from the regrettable incident of the low-heeled shoes, duly escaped from Innsbrück and was sent to Rome as the maid of the Duchess of Parma. Prince Sobiesky was exiled to Passau by the Emperor for his complicity in the business, and was also deprived of a couple of valuable duchies. Wogan, who had always been something of a poet, devoted the remainder of his life to the cultivation of the Muse, his efforts drawing encomiums from so severe a critic as Dean Swift, to whom he had sent a copy of his verses in "a bag of green velvet embroidered in gold." He died in 1747.

As for the Princess, her wedded life did not fulfil the romantic promise of its beginnings. Married to a worthy but doleful husband, she never sat on the throne which she had been promised. She was the mother of Prince Charles Edward, and seems to have fallen into delicate health, for in one of his boyish letters the little Prince promises not to jump or make a noise so as to "disturb mamma."

Prince James.

XII

ON THE ROOF OF THE WORLD

THE land between the deserts of Turkestan and the plains of India and between the Persian plateau and China still remains the least known and the most difficult on the globe. There are to be found the highest mountains in the world—a confusion of mighty snow-clad ranges varied by icy uplands and deep-cut, inaccessible valleys. Old roads cross it which have been caravan routes since the days of Alexander the Great, but these roads are few and far between. One, perhaps the most famous, goes from Kashmir across the Indus and over the Karakoram Pass to Khotan and Yarkand. That pass is 18,500 feet, the highest in the world which still serves the purpose of an avenue of trade.

This wild upland is not the place where one would look for hurried journeys. The country is too intricate, the inhabitants are too few, and there man's life seems a trifling thing against the background of eternal ice. Yet I have heard of two long, stubborn chases in that no-man's-land, the tale of which is worth telling.

I

The first concerns the Karakoram Pass. Till the other day, on the cairn which marked the summit, there lay a marble slab engraved with a man's name. It recorded a murder which took place in that outlandish spot in the year 1880.

At that time there was in those parts a young Scotsman called Dalgleish, who used to accompany travellers and hunters on their expeditions. He was also a trader, making long journeys across Central Asia, and in his business had dealings with a certain Pathan called Dad Mahomed Khan. This Pathan had been a trader and a bit of a smuggler, and was well known on the road between Yarkand and Ladakh. The two used to have ventures together, and were apparently good friends.

A year or two before Dalgleish had gone off on a long expedition into Tibet, and in his absence things went badly with Dad Mahomed. All his ponies were destroyed in a storm in the passes, and this compelled him to resort to Hindu money-lenders. Luck continued obstinately against him, and he found himself unable to repay his loans. The result was that his creditors brought the matter before the British Commissioner at Leh, and he was forbidden to trade on the Yarkand-Leh road until he had paid his debts.

The upshot was that the Pathan fell into evil ways, and Dalgleish, when he returned from his expedition, found him living at Leh in idleness and poverty. Desiring to help his old colleague, Dalgleish invited him to join him, and tried to get the Commissioner to withdraw the injunction. But the Commissioner refused, so Dalgleish set off alone for the north with a small caravan. On the way he halted and wrote back to Dad Mahomed, asking him to follow him. This the Pathan did, and the two continued on the long road up the Karakoram Pass. Dalgleish gave Dad Mahomed a tent and a riding horse, and instructed his servants to treat him as they treated himself.

They camped north of the Karakoram Pass, and one afternoon were observed to walk out together, the

Pathan carrying Dalgleish's rifle. Then came the sound of a shot, but the servants took no notice, as game was plentiful around the camp. Presently, however, Dad Mahomed returned and informed them that he had shot the Sahib. The servants ran to their master, and Dad Mahomed followed, having provided himself with a tulwar. Dalgleish was only wounded in the shoulder, and the Pathan then attacked him and brutally murdered him. He drove back the servants to their tent, warning them that if they left it he would kill them.

Dad Mahomed took possession of Dalgleish's tent, and in the morning ordered the horses to be loaded and the caravan to proceed. At the end of the next stage he told the servants that they could do what they liked with the merchandise, and he himself rode off on Dalgleish's horse. What the motive for the murder was it is impossible to say; it could not have been robbery, for Dalgleish had a large sum in notes which was found untouched. The servants took the caravan back to the Karakoram Pass, picked up Dalgleish's body, and returned to Leh.

The British Raj now took up the case. Dad Mahomed was found guilty of murder, and a large reward was offered for his capture. But to find a Pathan who had had many days' start in Central Asia was like looking for a needle in a haystack. Nevertheless, it was essential for British prestige that the murderer should be found.

Colonel Bower, the well-known traveller, was at that time at Kashgar, where he received a letter from the Indian Government bidding him arrest Dad Mahomed at all costs and bring him back to India for trial. It appeared that Dad Mahomed had been recently in Kashgar boasting of his deed. The Chinese authorities did not molest him, and it was found impossible to entice him inside the grounds of the Russian Consulate.

Colonel Bower's mission was kept a profound secret. The Pathan appeared to have left Kashgar, going east, some weeks before. A Hindu merchant was discovered who had a bitter hatred of the murderer, and plans were concerted. Emissaries were sent throughout Central Asia to make inquiry. They were furnished with letters explaining their purpose, but these letters were only to be used when they found their man; otherwise their inquiries must be made secretly, and they had to pose as ordinary travellers.

Two of them went into Afghanistan, a troublesome country to journey in. They were arrested in Balkh, and declared that they were doctors looking for rare plants. Fortunately the Amir, Abdur Rahman, happened to be close at hand, and the two men asked to be taken before him. They gave him Colonel Bower's letter to read, and the Amir smiled grimly. These men, he told his entourage, are honest and are what they profess to be. They will not, however, find the plant they seek in Afghanistan; but, he added, he had heard that it grew in Bokhara. The two were released and given presents of money and clothes.

Colonel Bower himself had gone east from Kashgar, on the trail which the Pathan was believed to have taken. One day a man came to his camp and asked his nationality. Bower said he came from India, and his visitor expressed his astonishment, for he thought that the people of India were black. He added that in the neighbourhood there was another foreigner, and nobody knew where he came from—a tall man not unlike the Sahib. He lived in the jungle and earned money by wood-cutting. This convinced Bower that he was on the track of the fugitive, but when he reached the place mentioned his man was gone. The news of the arrival of an Englishman from India had been enough for Dad Mahomed.

Months passed and nothing happened, and Colonel Bower had begun to think his task hopeless, when suddenly there came news from Samarkand that the Pathan had been caught there and was now in a Russian prison. Two of the emissaries who had gone in that direction had arrived in Samarkand, and had found Dad Mahomed sitting on a box in the bazaar. One of them stopped and engaged him in conversation, while the other went off to the Governor, who happened to be the famous General Kuropatkin. Kuropatkin, on opening Bower's letter, at once sent a party of Cossacks to the bazaar and had Dad Mahomed arrested.

It was arranged to send him to India, and preparations were made for an armed escort to bring him back over the Russian border; but news arrived that the criminal had cheated justice, for he had hung himself in his cell. Nevertheless the power of the British law was vindicated, and the story of the unrelenting pursuit throughout Central Asia had an immense moral effect in all that mountain country. The tale of it was repeated at camp-fires and bazaars everywhere between Persia and China, till the Great War, with its far wilder romances, came to dim its memory.

II

The break-up of Russia after the Bolsheviks seized the Government had extraordinary results in every part of the old Russian Empire, but in none more extraordinary than in the Central Asian Provinces. It was like some strange chemical dropped into an innocent compound and altering every constituent. The old cradle of the Aryan races was in an uproar. In the ancient khanates of Bokhara and Samarkand—names sung in poetry for two thousand years—strange governments arose, talking half-understood Western communism. Everywhere the ferment was felt; in Tashkend, in Yarkand, in Afghanistan, in the Pamirs, and along the Indian border. Austrian and

German prisoners set free in Siberia were trying to fight their way towards the Caspian; tribes of brigands seized the occasion for guerilla warfare and general looting; and Bolshevik propaganda penetrated by strange channels through the passes into India. The Armistice in Europe made very little difference to this pandemonium. Central Asia was in a confusion which it had scarcely known since the days of Tamerlane.

In this witches' sabbath of disaster appeared one or two British officers striving to keep the King's peace on and beyond the frontier. One of these, Captain L. V. S. Blacker, had been badly wounded in the Flying Corps in France. Then he rejoined his old regiment, the Guides; and in July 1918 was in Tashkend looking after British interests in the face of a parody of Government which called itself a Soviet. After that he made his way south into the Pamirs and fetched up at Tashkurghan, on one of the sources of the Yarkand River. He had with him seven men of the Guides.

There he heard from an Afghan merchant that about a hundred armed men—Afghans, but probably led by Germans and Turks—had been seen in the upper gorges of the Tashkurghan River.* This matter required looking into. Having only seven men he went to the little Russian fort adjoining and succeeded in borrowing twelve Cossacks. The place was in the Chinese Pamirs and the local Amban was troublesome about horses, but Captain Blacker managed to raise sufficient from Hindu traders. Mounted on their ponies, and with a single pack-horse carrying rations, the expedition started by descending the river till a place was found where it could be forded. They reached the spot where the enemy band had been last heard of, but found no tracks on the goat-

* Captain Blacker has told this story in his excellent book *On Secret Patrol in High Asia* (John Murray), one of the best narratives of adventure published in recent years.

path leading up to the high passes. But this was probably the direction of the enemy, so they crossed the ridge which divided their valley from Taghdumbash.

It was late October and bitterly cold on the high hills. At a village called Wacha they still found no tracks of the band, so they halted there and sent out patrols along the possible routes. Next morning they decided that the Cossacks should stop at Wacha, while Captain Blacker and his Guides crossed the ridge back to Taghdumbash to try and pick up the trail. Their journey took them over a high pass, called "The Thieves' Pass," and as the weather was fine their spirits rose. Still there was no sign of the enemy, and they were compelled to go back to Tashkurghan and spend the night there in a house.

Early next morning they started again for Dafdar, and covered the forty miles thither in eight hours. In these high latitudes even a Kirghiz pony cannot manage more than five miles an hour. At Dafdar they hunted up the Beg and from him they had news. Fifteen wild-looking strangers, mounted on big horses and with rifles at their backs, had several nights before ridden through the village, and a shepherd had recently seen their tracks in a patch of snow. Clearly it was the gang who had come from the Russian Pamirs, for ordinary traders do not travel in that guise, or, indeed, travel these roads at all in early winter. They might be opium smugglers, or smugglers of Bolshevik propaganda, or enemy agents commissioned to make trouble in North India. Anyhow, it was Captain Blacker's business to round them up and make certain.

That night he sent one of his N.C.O.s sixteen miles up the valley on the road to India, where there was a post of the Gilgit Scouts, with instructions to beg half a dozen rifles and a pony-load of barley meal. The rendezvous was fixed on the Ili-Su upland. Next morning, accordingly, the expedition was joined by half a dozen men of the Scouts—a wild lot with their Dard caps, and their long hair, and their untanned leggings. The Gilgit Scouts did not bother with transport, but came with what they stood up in. Ten screws from Dafdar were commandeered and loads were made up; and, says Captain Blacker, "each man strapped his sheepskin coat and a blanket to the strait saddle-tree of the Pamir, filled his mess-tin and his oil bottle, thrust a length of '4 by 2' in his haversack, and was ready for an eight-hundred mile hunt through desolation."

The weather had changed and the leaden sky promised snow. All around were the snowy Mustagh peaks, rising to 25,000 feet and more, while before lay a wind-swept icy tableland. It was hard going in such weather, and they took five hours to reach the banks of the Oprang River. There they found a Kirghiz encampment, and learned from them that, seven nights before, fifteen well-mounted men had filed past the tents in the darkness. A night was spent in the encampment, and there arrived the N.C.O. who had been sent to the post of the Gilgit Scouts, bringing with him ponies and part of the barley meal.

It was snowing in the morning, and pushing up the Ili-Su valley they found on the shale of the ravines clearly marked tracks of men. It was a severe climb, for the slopes were ice-coated, and the ponies had to be dragged up to the crest of the pass. On the top once more they came on the prints of men and horses —prints which they were to know pretty exactly during the next fourteen days. The pass of Ili-Su was some 17,000 feet. The farther valley proved very rough; but late in the afternoon it opened out, and the night was spent in wet snow under a cliff, where enough brushwood could be found to make a fire. Every night it was necessary to cook enough barley scones to serve for the next day.

The following morning the snow was falling resolutely, but they pursued the course down the steep banks of the stream. The enemy tracks were still clear, and it was plain that their mounts were the big horses of Badakshan. The band had a long start, and the only chance of catching them up was to start very early and finish very late—no light task in such weather and in such a country. Farther down the valley they found the ashes of a fire and a new china tea-cup lately broken in half, with, on the bottom, the legend "Made in Japan." It was certain now that they were on the right road; for Kirghiz shepherds do not own china cups. Where was the band heading? Not for India—probably for Yarkand; possibly for some place still farther east. It was therefore necessary for Captain Blacker to turn south-east up the Raskam River, and plunge into the wild tangle of the Karakoram mountains.

After eight hours' hard going they came to a place called Hot Springs, where once more they found traces of their quarry, some horses' droppings, a heap of pigeons' feathers, and some empty cartridge cases. After that the cliff sides closed in and they struggled for hours in the darkness through a narrow gorge, till they came to a place at a lower altitude where there were brushwood for fire and grass to cut for bedding.

Off again next morning; still up the Raskam valley with the great buttresses of the Kuen-lun on the north bank, and far away on the right the slopes of the Mustagh. If the tracks led up the river bank the enemy was bound for Khotan; if across the stream, for Yarkand. Apparently they crossed, and it was no easy matter following them, for the river was swollen with snow. On the other side with some difficulty they picked up the trail again, and found it moving towards the slopes of the Kuen-lun. Clearly the enemy was bound for Yarkand or Karghalik.

They had a tough climb to the top of the pass, and once more the trackers were at fault. Some tracks led eastward to the edge of a dizzy precipice, which was clearly not the way. Others, however, plunged down a slope into a gorge full of thorns, and there they discovered traces of the enemy's bivouac. This was at midday, which showed that the pursuit was gaining.

In the afternoon they fought their way through a tangle of undergrowth till they arrived at a Kirghiz encampment, where they managed to buy barley. In one tent they found a young Kirghiz lad whom they took along with them as a guide. As it turned out, his father was guiding the enemy.

The expedition was now in better spirits, for they had food in their saddle-bags and knew that they were not bound for the icy deserts of the Karakoram. Down a little north-running valley they went, and again they came upon dung, which they judged to be five days old. The tracks led down the valley, and suddenly ceased abruptly. Was it possible that the gang were hiding in the neighbouring brushwood? They beat the place in vain, and were compelled to return the way they had come. Then they discovered a narrow cleft in the rocks, which proved to be the mouth of a side valley, and in it they again came on the trail.

The night was spent on a tiny patch of grass under the cliffs, while their meal was of girdle cakes made with the newly bought barley, and some of the last of their tea. "A cheerful spot," says Captain Blacker, "but better, at any rate, than the trenches before La Bassée in February 1915."

Next day they still climbed, and at midday found more relics of the enemy, a copper kettle, a cauldron, and a goatskin full of butter, which had apparently been too heavy to carry. Then they crossed a very lofty snow-pass, and before them saw the steep ranges of the Kuen-lun. Down one ridge and up another they went, still following the track, and at one stopping-place they found a dead quail and a straw cage This proved that there was at least one Pathan in the gang, for it is the Pathan's endearing habit to carry tame birds in the folds of his raiment.

They were now in a perfectly desolate upland without grass or water or fuel, and their food was rapidly failing. They had one and a half day's rations in hand, consisting only of barley flour and a very little tea and sugar. A lucky shot by Captain Blacker at a young burhal the day before had given them some meat, but this was all they had had for a week. The country, too, was becoming desperately rocky. If the Pamirs was the roof of the world, it seemed to Captain Blacker that he was now climbing among the chimney-pots. Sometimes on the summit of a pass they had to dig a way for the ponies with hands and bayonets. The ponies, too, began to die.

At last, after several days' severe labour, they descended from the heights to gentler elevations, and found Kirghiz encampments, where they could get fresh barley and now and then a sheep. They were on the lower foot-hills of the Kuen-lun now, and were looking again at fields and crops. They were able also to acquire fresh horses. Up a long valley they went, still finding traces of the enemy's bivouacs. They had to stop sometimes to mend their footgear with yak's hide ; and they had now and then a piece of luck, as when they came to the house of a certain Kirghiz Beg, who lent them guides. Once again they had mountains to cross, lower passes but rockier, and breaking down into deep gorges. Often they marched fifteen hours in a day.

At last they reached a village where they had intelligence of the enemy. They learned that the gang were only forty-eight hours ahead, which meant that they had gained five or six days on them in the last eight. The destination was clearly Yarkand, and there was always a risk of losing them in that city. Here, too, the trail gave out, for the sheep and goats of the villagers had smothered it, so they had to hire a guide.

But the way he led them showed no tracks. They could only push on and hope to cut the trail again from the eastward. After crossing a pass of 15,000 feet they came to a narrow valley, which led them to the river Pokhpu, running north and south. No vestige of a trail, however, could be found on its banks, so they forded the stream and ascended a gorge upon the other side. This took them over a 15,000 feet ridge and down into another valley and then into another. It ended in a gigantic chasm, where in the moonlight a huge excrescence of rock showed exactly like an ace of spades. Captain Blacker took this for a good omen; but there was still a fourth pass to cross, and at four in the morning the expedition flung itself down, utterly exhausted, in a waterless valley called after the Angel Gabriel. In that single day's march they had climbed up and down something like 30,000 feet, from seven o'clock of one morning to four o'clock of the next.

The ace of spades had not misled them, for soon after they started they met an old Kirghiz—a Hadji by his green turban. He was rather taken aback by the sight of them, but said he had been sent by a Chinese mandarin to meet a certain guest. This made Captain Blacker suspicious, so he boldly answered that he was the guest in question. The old Hadji was added to the party, and conducted them to the village of Kokyar, where they had at last a reasonable meal.

At midnight again they were off, after five hours' sleep, marching north-eastward by the compass, and hoping to get back on the trail they had lost. Presently they were among the sand-dunes of a desert, and then among the irrigation channels of the lower Raskam

River. It was midnight when they found themselves in the latter labyrinth; so Captain Blacker ordered the Hadji to find some one without delay who would show him the way out. It was an unfortunate step, for it landed them in a leper-house. There was nothing for it but to march on through the night, and in the small hours of the next morning they were within sight of Yarkand.

There, early in the afternoon, the expedition, now lean, weather-beaten, and tattered to the last degree, stood outside the ancient walls of Yarkand. One of the Guides entered the city, disguised, to find an acquaintance, from whom he heard to his delight that a party of wild-looking strangers had entered the streets eighteen hours before. Indeed, the man knew where they were. They were now in the Sarai Badakshan. Captain Blacker had not ridden hard for a fortnight among the wildest mountains on earth to stand on ceremony in any town. His sixteen men cantered down the alleys of Yarkand, and presently flung open the gates of the Sarai.

There the quarry was found. Every hand in the Sarai went up without delay when its inmates heard the challenge, and saw behind the gleaming bayonets the sixteen gaunt, wolfish faces of their pursuers.

EPILOGUE—ON RE-READING THE STORIES

(*For which the Author is not responsible.*)

I. The Flight to Varennes

1. Recall the events in France between 1789 and 1791.
2. The episode of the Queen's wrong turning gave Thomas Carlyle material for a stirring paragraph in his *French Revolution*. Here it is :—

Alas ! and the false Chambermaid has warned Gouvion that she thinks the Royal Family will fly this very night ; and Gouvion, distrusting his own glazed eyes, has sent express for Lafayette ; and Lafayette's Carriage, flaring with lights, rolls this moment through the inner Arch of the Carrousel,—where a Lady shaded in broad gypsy-hat, and leaning on the arm of a servant, also of the Runner or Courier sort, stands aside to let it pass, and has even the whim to touch a spoke of it with her *badine*,—light little magic rod which she calls *badine*, such as the Beautiful then wore. The flare of Lafayette's Carriage rolls past : all is found quiet in the Court-of-Princes ; sentries at their post ; Majesties' Apartments closed in smooth rest. Your false Chambermaid must have been mistaken ? Watch thou, Gouvion, with Argus' vigilance ; for, of a truth, treachery is within these walls.

But where is the Lady that stood aside in gypsy-hat and touched the wheel-spoke with her *badine* ? O Reader, that Lady that touched the wheel-spoke was the Queen of France ! She has issued safe through that inner Arch, into the Carrousel itself ; but not into the Rue de l'Echelle. Flurried by the rattle and rencounter, she took the right hand, not the left ; neither she nor her Courier knows Paris ; he indeed is no Courier, but a loyal stupid *ci-devant* Bodyguard disguised as one. They are off, quite wrong, over the Pont Royal and River; roaming disconsolate in the Rue du Bac; far from the Glass-coachman, who still waits.

3. Make a sketch-map showing the places mentioned in this story.
4. Which do you consider the most dramatic moment of this story, and which is the best pen-picture?
5. Justify (or criticize) the sentence on page 22: "It was the crisis of the French monarchy."
6. What might have happened if the royal party had escaped?
7. Note the simplicity of the telling of this story.
8. Read "Drouet's Ride" and "Mr. Barr's Annoyance" in *The Eye-Witness*, by Hilaire Belloc.

II. The Railway Raid in Georgia

1. Note the following facts:—

The American Civil War began in 1861 and lasted until 1865, and it is often spoken of as the War of Secession. The two parties were the Federals and the Confederates, the former being, generally speaking, the people of the Northern States, and the latter those of the Southern States. In the Southern States negro slaves were still employed on the cotton and sugar plantations, and the people of the Northern States objected to slavery being permitted within the American territories. The dispute went on for a long time before actual fighting commenced, and the Southerners proposed that they should form a separate Confederacy, in which the employment of negro slaves should be permitted. They wished to "secede" from the Union, and the Northerners objected to this.

The chief figure in the war on the Federal side was Abraham Lincoln, who became President. He did all he could to prevent war, and pleaded earnestly with the Southerners to "save the Union." But the dispute came to blows in April 1861, when the Confederates attacked Fort Sumter in the harbour of Charleston city in South Carolina. Lincoln made an appeal for fighting men, and some five million Northerners volunteered for active service.

The Confederates were, however, better prepared for the coming fight, and had better military leaders, and at the battle of Bull Run, near Washington, the Federals were beaten, while Lincoln found it difficult to prevent the occupation of the capital by the Southern troops. It was at the battle of Bull Run that Jackson, the Confederate leader, gained his nickname of Stonewall. His leader, General Lee, called out to his men, "Look at Jackson's brigade standing like a stone wall!"

After a time the Northerners found a capable leader in General Ulysses Grant, and the war went on with varying fortune. There was a battle of six days' duration at Chancellorsville, which ended in the repulse of the Federals. Stonewall Jackson was mortally wounded in this fight. A few days later he died. "Pass the infantry to the front," he called out with his dying breath. "Tell Major Hawks—" He lay for a few minutes and then added quietly, "Let us cross over the river and rest under the shade of the trees."

At Gettysburg, in July 1863, Lee was decisively defeated by General Mead, to the great joy of the Northerners. The struggle dragged on for two years longer, until Lee surrendered to General Grant in April 1865.

2. Trace the movement of this story on a map of the United States.
3. Which paragraph on page 28 gives the subject of this story?
4. Which names on page 32 are as important in the story as that of Andrews?
5. Which do you consider the crisis of the tale? Which are the most anxious moments?
6. Why did Andrews' exploit fail?

III. The Escape of King Charles after Worcester

1. Draw a sketch-map to include the places mentioned in this story.

2. Why does the writer change from the past to the present tense at the foot of page 47?
3. What are the critical points in this story?
4. Would this story make a good play, or a film?
5. Dramatize two of the conversational portions.
6. Is it correct to describe the hero as "King"?

IV. From Pretoria to the Sea

1. Prepare a sketch-map, inserting names, as you read the story for the second time.
2. Write a paragraph comparing Churchill's escape with that of King Charles.
3. Make a sketch showing Churchill's actual escape.
4. Which men named in the story would the fugitives be most delighted to meet?
5. What are the tensest moments of this story?

V. The Escape of Prince Charles Edward

1. Which sentence on page 81 gives the reason for the pursuit of Prince Charles after the Jacobite rising had been utterly broken?
2. Are there any points of likeness or difference between the adventures of King Charles and Prince Charlie?
3. Can you explain why we are nearly always glad when a hunted person escapes?
4. Re-read the whole story and make a list of those incidents which would make the best pictures for a film. Give a good title to the film.
5. Who are the leading persons in this story? Who are the chief secondary persons?
6. How would you describe the background of the drama?
7. Dramatize two or three of the critical episodes.

VI. Two African Journeys

1. Make a sketch-map to go with this story.
2. Give a good title to the first of these stories.
3. Select the sentence which shows the historic importance of King's ride.
4. Debate the question of the white man's right to displace the native.

VII. The Great Montrose

1. Study the following historical note :—

Early in 1638 it was decided to revive the National Covenant, which had been originally drawn up in 1557, and had been renewed in the reign of James VI. The nobles met in Edinburgh and signed the Covenant in Greyfriars' Church on the last day of February. They pledged themselves to maintain Protestantism, and claimed the right to settle their own form of religion without interference from England. The National Covenant was signed in many parts of Scotland as well as in Edinburgh; but it must not be thought that the whole nation was unanimous. There was always an Episcopalian party, strongest in the western Highlands and in the north-east of Scotland. In Aberdeen, for example, men were compelled to sign the Covenant against their will, for the young Earl of Montrose, at the head of an army, insisted on their doing so.

In Edinburgh and the south the Covenanters were very strong, and Charles I. had to agree to permit the meeting of a General Assembly. It met at Glasgow in November 1638, and when the King's commissioner, the Marquis of Hamilton, found out how determined it was, he dissolved it in the name of the King. The members refused to admit that the King had the right to dissolve a court of the church, and declared that Presbyterianism was to be the established religion of Scotland.

2. Draw a sketch-map to show the flank march described on page 143 and following pages.
3. Why is a figure of General Leslie placed at the end of this story?

4. Why does Montrose gain the reader's sympathy irrespective of the issues at stake.
5. Which do you consider the least creditable part of Montrose's exploits?

VIII. The Flight of Lieutenants Parer and McIntosh across the World

1. Draw a sketch-map of the world and mark in the routes mentioned in this story.
2. Think of a good motto for these two airmen.
3. Was their flight really "of no use to any one"?

IX. Lord Nithsdale's Escape

1. Study the following historical note:—

Queen Anne died in 1714. The Jacobites, or followers of King James, had hoped that she would recognize her half-brother as James III. of England and VIII. of Scotland. But she died without doing so, and the Elector of Hanover, a great-grandson of James VI. and I., succeeded to the throne without opposition. In the following year the followers of Prince James made their first great effort to put him on the throne. The Earl of Mar raised the standard at Braemar in August 1715, and soon a Jacobite army occupied Perth, and was preparing to march on Stirling and Edinburgh. The Duke of Argyll was sent to meet him, and an indecisive battle was fought at Sheriffmuir, near Dunblane, on November 13th.

Sheriffmuir was really a Hanoverian victory, for Argyll prevented Mar from marching southwards, and compelled him to return to Perth. The Jacobites in the north of England had been easily crushed at Preston about the same time as their Scottish allies were fighting at Sheriffmuir, and when James landed at Peterhead, in December, his cause was already hopeless. He was a brave man, of good private character, and he would have made a better and perhaps a wiser king than his obstinate and cruel father. But he was not the man to give life and enthusiasm to crestfallen and despairing troops, and he fled to France in the beginning of

February. Mar escaped with him, but three of the other leaders—Lords Kenmure, Derwentwater, and Nithsdale —were sentenced to death.

2. Which do you consider the most critical moment of this escape ?

X. Sir Robert Cary's Ride to Edinburgh

1. Draw a map of the Border to illustrate Cary's record of service in that region.
2. What was the motive of Cary's ride ? How does it differ from that which prompted other "hurried journeys" ?

XI. The Escape of Princess Clementina

1. This story is the basis of A. E. W. Mason's novel, *Clementina*.
2. John Sobiesky was elected king of Poland in 1674. In 1683 the Turks attacked Vienna, but were routed by Sobiesky and the Duke of Lorraine at the head of a Polish and German force.
3. Draw a sketch-map to accompany this story. Mark the most critical point of the journey.

XII. On the Roof of the World

1. Make a sketch-map to accompany this story.
2. Why are the reader's sympathies with the hunters in these two stories ?

Rearrange the stories of this book in chronological order. Which do you consider the finest story?

THE END

PRINTED IN GREAT BRITAIN AT
THE PRESS OF THE PUBLISHERS